COMPUTER ETHICS ETIQUETTE & SAFETY

For the 21st-Century Student

Nancy E. Willard

Computer Ethics, Etiquette, and Safety for the 21st-Century Student

Nancy E. Willard

Director of Publishing
Jean Marie Hall

Acquisitions Editors
Anita MacAnear
Matthew Manweller

Book Publishing Project Manager
Tracy Cozzens

Special Projects Manager
Diannah Anavir

Administrative Assistant
Pam Calegari

Illustrator
Michael Novotny

Copy Editor
Ron Renchler, The Electronic Page

Cover Design
Katherine Getta, Getta Graphic Design

Design and Production
Katherine Getta, Getta Graphic Design

International Society for Technology in Education (ISTE)
480 Charnelton Street
Eugene, OR 97401-2626
Order Desk: 800.336.5191
Order Fax: 541.302.3778
Customer Service: orders@iste.org
Books and Courseware: books@iste.org
World Wide Web: www.iste.org

First Edition
ISBN 1-56484-184-7

About ISTE

The International Society for Technology in Education (ISTE) is a nonprofit professional organization with a worldwide membership of leaders in educational technology. We are dedicated to promoting appropriate uses of information technology to support and improve learning, teaching, and administration in K–12 education and teacher education. As part of that mission, ISTE provides high-quality and timely information, services, and materials, such as this book.

ISTE's Publishing Department works with experienced educators to develop and produce classroom-tested books and courseware. We look for content that emphasizes the use of technology where it can make a difference—making the teacher's job easier; saving time; motivating students; helping students who have unique learning styles, abilities, or backgrounds; and creating learning environments that would be impossible without technology. We believe technology can improve the effectiveness of teaching while making learning exciting and fun.

Every manuscript and product we select for publication is peer reviewed and professionally edited. While we take pride in our publications, we also recognize the difficulties of maintaining quality while keeping on top of the latest technologies and research. Please let us know what products you would find helpful. We value your feedback on this book and other ISTE products. E-mail us at **books@iste.org**.

ISTE is home of the National Educational Technology Standards (NETS) Project and the National Center for Preparing Tomorrow's Teachers to Use Technology (NCPT^3). To learn more about NETS or request a print catalog, visit our Web site at **www.iste.org**, which provides:

- Current educational technology standards for K–12 student and teacher education
- A bookstore with online ordering and membership discount options
- *Learning & Leading with Technology* magazine
- *ISTE Update*, membership newsletter
- Teacher resources
- Discussion groups
- Professional development services, including national conference information
- Research projects
- Member services

About the Author

Nancy Willard has written extensively on legal and policy issues related to the use of the Internet in schools. These resources are available on the Responsible Netizen Web site at http://netizen.uoregon.edu. Her approach to these issues is grounded in her personal and professional background. She has been a teacher of children with behavior problems, an attorney with a focus on computer and copyright law, and a consultant to school districts regarding the planning and implementation of technology. Most recently, Nancy has initiated a research program that seeks to understand the factors influencing moral development and ethical decision making in an information technology environment.

About the Illustrator

Michael Novotny is a 21-year-old art student from Portland, Oregon. He is currently studying graphic design and working toward his animation certificate. He illustrated his first book in 1998. Michael has experimented with cartoon and media styles in producing advertisements and flyers for music groups in the Portland area. Michael hopes to reach out to the community with his art by creating illustrations for educational books.

Foreword

The world is wired. Computers control and dominate the infrastructure we take for granted. The delivery of electricity, the air traffic control system, the telephone system, emergency services (911), and retail sales are just a few of the areas that are almost completely dependent on computers to function correctly. In our personal lives the Internet has become an indispensable resource. The phenomenal growth of this medium is testimony to its multiple uses and broad acceptance. E-mail, instant messaging, research, and entertainment are but a few of the ways in which networked computers enhance our lives.

Our children have moved to the wired environment with little hesitation. They have become the experts, in many cases teaching their parents and teachers how the Internet operates. Older generations used computers as tools focusing on problem solving (spreadsheets), communication (word processing), and presentation (graphics). Our children are living in a networked world. Children today have more computer power at their fingertips than did entire nations only two generations ago. Our children are explorers using their computers as a magic carpet to discover far-off lands, find new friends, enhance their knowledge, and, yes, get into trouble.

The focus we have taken with our children with respect to computers and the Internet has been twofold—teaching the technology and stressing online safety. Both these issues are well understood. The problem is that there is a third issue that is generally forgotten in our haste to preach technology and safety. That important third issue is ethics. How are our children being taught to behave online? How many parents ever give a thought to their child's online behavior? The answer is—not many. Research conducted by the Cybercitizen Partnership indicates that most parents do not ever consider that their children could be committing computer crime when they illegally download the copyrighted works of others, cause disruption and destruction by defacing Web sites, engage in hate speech, or break into other computers, either for fun or profit.

Nancy Willard has been a leader in the effort to develop tools for teaching appropriate online behavior. *Computer Ethics, Etiquette, and Safety for the 21st-Century Student* continues that effort. Recognizing that there are factors at work in the virtual world that are not easily duplicated in the real world, Nancy focuses on basic behavioral issues in order to match situations with behavioral forces. Recognizing that there can be misunderstandings on the very question of what is right and what is wrong, she uses concrete examples that teachers and parents can rely on to deliver this important message. As a member of the Cybercitizen Advisory Council, Nancy has been instrumental in assisting the organization in developing an action plan to reach parents, teachers, and kids. This book is another valuable resource in that effort.

The standard solution to network protection today is more and better security products. While effective to a point, this strategy has resulted in a virtual arms race, with the attackers ultimately defeating a security tool and thus beginning another cycle of protect-and-attack. Teaching users to behave ethically online will help reduce the escalating problem of computer crime and mischief.

Make no mistake—we are talking about an ongoing, concerted effort that will require parents, teachers, corporations, and institutions to work together to create a generation of ethical cybercitizens. Nancy Willard's book is an important part of that battle.

Peter N. Smith
Director, Cybercitizen Partnership

Contents

Teacher's Introduction

The Master said,

"If you govern the people legalistically and control them by punishment, they will avoid crime, but have no personal sense of shame.

If you govern them by means of virtue and control them with propriety, they will gain their own sense of shame, and thus correct themselves."

From *Confucian Analects*, 500 B.C., www.human.toyogakuen-u.ac.jp/~acmuller/contao/analects.htm

If Confucius was right, then today's students will need guidance in understanding the ethics required by an advanced technological society. This introduction is designed to explain how *Computer Ethics, Etiquette, and Safety for the 21st-Century Student* can help teachers facilitate student understanding of the rules that govern ethical computer use.

This book can also be a complement to your school's Internet use policy and other technology policies. Its primary purpose is to provide students with a greater understanding of the reasons for your school's rules.

To address the question of how to help young people use information and communication technologies ethically, we must consider how young people learn to engage in ethical behavior. Furthermore, we must examine how information and communication technologies and the emerging cyber environment can affect their learning and behavior.

Some Essential Questions

How do young people learn to engage in ethical behavior?

In 2000, I presented at a conference on cyberethics hosted by the Information Technology Association of America and the U.S. Department of Justice. At the conference, the keynote speaker was Patricia Wallace, author of *Psychology of the Internet*. She mentioned a research study by Batson and others that assessed influences on honest behavior. One of the interventions the researchers used was the placement of a freestanding mirror in the room with the subject. The mere placement of this mirror resulted in a significantly higher level of honest behavior.

Later that day at the conference, a member of the audience for a panel I was on posed a question: "If you were king or queen for a day, what one thing would you do to enhance ethical behavior in the use of the Internet?" The answer that immediately popped into my mind was: "I would install a small mirror on every computer so that more people would understand that what they do on the Internet reflects upon who they are as a person." My second thought was: "Wow, I just found the new title to the first unit of my book!"

As young people grow, their emerging cognitive development enables them to gain increasingly accurate perceptions of the world around them. Three principal external influences combine with this emerging cognitive development to affect moral development and behavior. These factors are:

1. **A recognition that an action has caused harm.** When a young person engages in inappropriate action and recognizes that his or her action has caused harm to another person, an empathic response occurs, leading to feelings of remorse.

2. **Social disapproval.** When a young person engages in inappropriate action and recognizes that others have become aware of and disapprove of this action, a "loss of face" and feelings of shame occur.

3. **Punishment by authority.** When a young person engages in an inappropriate action and a person with authority over the young person detects it, the punishment the person in authority imposes can lead to feelings of regret, but can also lead to anger at the person in authority.

These three external influences not only affect behavior in young people (and older people as well), they also play a major role in a young person's moral development. During adolescence, young people develop a sense of their own personal identity, and they incorporate an internalized personal moral code into it. In both adolescents and adults, a personal moral code functions as an internal influence for ethical and responsible behavior. Behavior is influenced both by external factors and the internalized moral code.

When we perceive that we have violated our own personal moral code, we feel guilty—unless we can rationalize our actions in some manner. We are all willing, under certain circumstances, to waver from our personal moral code; and we have an internalized limit to how far we are willing to waver from it. This limit protects against unlimited transgressions. The boundaries of this limit vary from person to person.

Several factors appear to influence our decision to waver from our personal moral code. We are more likely to waver when our assessment is that:

• There is an extremely limited chance or no chance of detection and punishment.

• The transgression will cause no perceptible harm.

• The harm may be perceptible but is small in comparison to the personal benefit we will gain.

• The harm is to a large entity, such as a corporation, and no specific or known person will suffer any loss.

- Many other people engage in such behavior, even though others may consider the behavior to be illegal or unethical.

- The entity or individual who is or could be harmed by the action has engaged in unfair or unjust actions.

How do information and communication technologies affect a young person's ethical behavior?

Information and communication technologies have a profound effect on the external influences of behavior. There are two significant characteristics of technology that influence behavior:

1. **Technology does not provide tangible feedback.** When people use technology, there is a lack of tangible feedback about the consequences of actions on others. People are distanced from a perception of the harm their behavior has caused. This lack of tangible feedback undermines the empathic response and thus undermines feelings of remorse. It then makes it easier to rationalize an action.

2. **Technology allows us to become invisible.** In fact, people are not totally invisible when they use the Internet. In most cases, they leave "cyberfootprints" wherever they go. But despite this reality the perception of invisibility persists. Some actions associated with technology are quite invisible, such as borrowing a friend's software program and installing it on your own computer. It is also possible to increase the level of invisibility by using technological tools. Establishing a pseudonymous account enhances invisibility. The fact that many people may be engaged in a similar activity also leads to a perception of invisibility because individual actions seem like such a "drop in the pond" that they are unlikely to be detected.

Invisibility undermines the potential influence of both authority and social disapproval. If a transgression cannot be detected and a person is unlikely to be punished, threats of punishment are not likely to have any effect whatsoever on behavior.

The issue of the effect of invisibility on human behavior is not new; Plato raised it in his story about the Ring of Gyges. In this story, a shepherd found a magical ring. When the stone was rotated, the shepherd became invisible. The story raises important questions: If we possessed the magic ring and were invisible, how would we choose to behave? Would we do whatever we wanted to do because we knew that nobody would catch and punish us? Would we do something that could hurt someone because we knew that nobody could tell who had done it, or would we do what we knew was right?

It is important to recognize that at the same time young people are using the Internet and being influenced by a lack of tangible feedback and by perceptions of invisibility, they are in the process of developing their internalized personal moral code. Unfortunately, we do not know how this set of circumstances will affect their development and internalization process.

What strategies can be used to address the influences of the lack of tangible feedback and the perception of invisibility when young people use information technologies?

There are several ways we can aid young people in using information technologies appropriately and ethically:

- **Help young people learn to do what is right regardless of the potential of detection and punishment.** We must shift our focus away from rules and threats of punishments and instead enhance young people's reliance on their own internalized personal moral code. Threats of punishment are simply an ineffective approach when the likelihood of detection and punishment is so remote. The message "Don't do this because it is against the rules" has limited impact if technology users believe they are invisible and their actions cannot or will not be detected and punished. Instead, we must focus young people's attention on the reasons for the rules. Rules are generally enacted because actions that violate the rules can cause harm to someone else. Thus, our focus must be on the potential harm, not the rule. In a world where we seem invisible, a much more powerful message is: "Don't do this, because if you do you will harm someone by (describe the possible harmful impact of the action)."

- **Help young people understand how actions can cause harm to people they can't see.** Empathy actually has two components: a feeling component and a thinking component. When we see or hear someone who is happy or sad, we begin to feel the same way inside. This is the feeling part of empathy. As young people grow, they also gain the ability to understand cognitively how other people think and feel. They learn to look at things from another person's perspective. This is the thinking part of empathy. Thinking about how someone else feels can also affect how we feel inside. The lack of tangible feedback in technology use impairs the feeling component of empathy. We must help young people learn to rely on the thinking part of empathy when they use information technologies.

- **Help young people learn to use effective decision-making strategies that will result in ethical and responsible behaviors.** These strategies must be effective even though young people do not have tangible feedback and may perceive themselves to be invisible when they use technology.

Eight Ethical Decision-Making Strategies

This book incorporates eight ethical decision-making strategies that can help young people learn to behave ethically and responsibly.

Golden Rule Test. How would you feel if others did the same thing to you that you did to them? If you would not want to have someone do the same thing to you, then the action is probably wrong.

A version of the Golden Rule is found in every religion in the world. Having students consider how they would feel if others did the same thing to them is a powerful ethical decision-making strategy.

Trusted Adult Test. What would your mom or dad, guardian, or other adult who is important in your life think? Your parents, guardians, or other adults who are important to you may not understand the Internet, but they know a lot about deciding whether an action is right or wrong. Considering how your parents, guardians, or other important adult would judge your actions will help you act in accordance with your family's values.

Philosophers call this the Moral Exemplar. Young people can be encouraged to model the behavior of those whose opinions are important to them. This test also brings in the importance of acting in accordance with the values that have been established by the family.

Is There a Rule? Test. Generally, rules or laws have been created to protect the rights of people and serve the common good. Rules and laws provide good guidance on whether or not an action is right or wrong.

It is important for young people to recognize the basis upon which rules have been created—to protect the rights of people and to serve the common good. The focus must always be on the reason for the rule, not the rule itself. This is a very important distinction. Young people may think that if they are invisible and no one can punish them for violating a rule, then the rule is of no importance.

Front Page Test. If your action were reported on the front page of the newspaper, what would other people think? One way to make good decisions is to act as if the whole world can see what you are doing.

The Front Page Test can help young people address their feelings of invisibility when using technology. There have been a number of widely reported incidents where an individual thought his or her actions were private only to find them ultimately reported on the front pages of various newspapers.

If Everybody Did It Test. What would happen if everybody made a decision to do the same thing you do? Consider what kind of world this would be if everyone did what you are thinking of doing. You might think that you are only causing a little bit of harm. But if everyone else also did a little bit of harm, then someone else might suffer a lot of hurt.

This test is an updated version of Kant's Moral Imperative. Encourage young people to consider the large amount of harm caused by many people engaging in small acts of harm.

Real World Test. Would it be okay if you did a particular action or similar action in the real world? Just because you do something in cyberspace does not mean that you cannot hurt someone. Actions in cyberspace can cause just as much harm to someone else as actions in the real world.

Considering their actions in the context of the real world can help young people create a better understanding of the consequences of actions on others. The Real World Test will help young people gain a better understanding of the real harm caused to real people.

Gandhi Test. Sometimes when people behave inappropriately on the Internet they claim that they are actually trying to make the Internet a better place. Mahatma Gandhi was a great leader in India who led a successful revolution using nonviolent resistance. One of the things he said was: "We must be the change we wish to see." It is a good thing for people to try to make the Internet and the world a better place, and you will be most successful in making things better if you behave in a way that you want others to behave.

Some of what is characterized as misbehavior on the Internet is the result of young people seeking to change what they perceive to be unethical or inappropriate behavior on the part of others. The target of such actions may be corporations or government agencies. Sometimes the target is local school officials.

Our messages to young people are not consistent when it relates to misbehavior that challenges the unethical or inappropriate behavior of others. We applaud the actions of the Revolutionaries who hacked their way on to British merchant ships and threw the tea overboard, but we criticize young people who hack corporate Web sites to post messages critical of a corporation's actions. Recognizing the importance of civil disobedience as a vehicle for creating positive change, this book seeks to help young people understand that they will be most effective in creating positive change when they uphold high ethical standards as they use the communication and information-sharing capabilities of the Internet to responsibly address issues they are concerned about.

Check Inside Test. How do you feel inside? We all have a "voice of conscience" inside of us that helps us figure out whether an action is right or wrong. If the inside of your body feels uncomfortable, the action is probably wrong. But if you have a feeling of peace and comfort inside, the action is probably right.

The Check-Inside Test is an ethical decision-making strategy that can help young people determine whether their actions reflect their internalized values. When our actions are invisible and we cannot directly witness the harm our actions may have caused, then our internal "voice of conscience" must be heard.

Technology Standards

Computer Ethics, Etiquette, and Safety for the 21st-Century Student specifically addresses the following National Educational Technology Standards (NETS) for Students developed by the International Society for Technology in Education (ISTE):

2. Social, ethical, and human issues

- Students understand the ethical, cultural, and societal issues related to technology.

- Students practice responsible use of technology systems, information, and software.

- Students develop positive attitudes toward technology uses that support lifelong learning, collaboration, personal pursuits, and productivity.

The National Science Foundation provided funding for the author's research study titled "Analysis of Information Technology Ethics Issues by High School Students," which provided insight into how young people make decisions regarding the ethical use of the Internet (Grant #SES-9818211). Insight gained through this research provided the foundation for the ethical decision-making approaches incorporated into this book.

How to Use This Book

This book is divided into 14 short units. Units 1 and 2 describe the overall ethical decision-making approach used throughout the book. It is essential that each student read Unit 1, "What You Do Reflects on You," before proceeding to any of the subsequent units. Unit 1 provides the ethical decision-making strategies and tools necessary to understand and use the rest of the book.

Each subsequent unit deals with one aspect of technology ethics. The units are typically two to three pages long and are written for a student audience. Units 3 through 14 can be introduced sequentially or introduced (or reused) at a "teachable moment." Each unit can be copied and given as a handout to students. (Yes, you have copyright permission to make copies for your own class!) After you introduce the unit topic, students should read the short handout. On a separate page at the end of each unit, you will find a set of short activities for the class. These activities include discussion questions, projects, role-playing scenarios, and more. We hope they are useful tools for teaching the ethics of technology use.

The units and activities in this book are intended for students in Grades 6-12. Later units deal with subject matter such as adult Web sites, Internet stalking, and Internet plagiarism.

The author has also established a "sharing place" on the Responsible Netizen Web site (http://netizen.uoregon.edu) to facilitate the exchange of additional learning activities. If you create any additional learning activities related to this book and wish to share them with others, you can submit them to this site.

.

UNIT 1

What You Do Reflects on You

Someone just gave you a magic ring. If you put this ring on, it will make you invisible. How will you choose to behave? Will you do whatever you want to do because you know that nobody can catch and punish you? Or will you do what you know is right? Consider this: Do you act the same way in a chat room as you do on the phone or in public?

where did he go?

When you use the Internet it can feel like you are invisible. It is just you, the keyboard, and the computer. You might think that you could do whatever you want. You may not worry about getting caught. You may not think about whether your actions might hurt someone else.

Are you really invisible when you use the Internet? Most of the time you are not. Computer systems do a good job of tracking computer use. You are actually leaving little "cyberfootprints" wherever you go. But because it feels like you are invisible, you might forget that your actions can be traced.

Regardless of whether or not you are invisible, consider how your actions reflect on the kind of person you are.

Are you a person who will do something you know is wrong because you think that nobody else will find out?

Or are you a person who will do what is right, even if you might be able to get away with doing something wrong?

When you use the Internet, your actions will reflect on the kind of person you are. Do you try to do what is right? Are you kind to other people, even strangers? Do you respect other people's property? Do you make safe choices for your own behavior and activities? Do you want to make a positive contribution to the world? If you answered "yes" to all of these questions, then the fact that you may feel that you are invisible on the Internet should have no impact on what you do.

Just Because You Can, Doesn't Make It Right

Sometimes it can be difficult to figure out whether an action is right or wrong. Just because you can do something doesn't make it right. Learning how to make the right choice all by yourself is an important part of growing up. Your parents, teachers, and other adults in your life can help you learn how to make the right choices. But, sooner or later, you are the one who will have to decide what is right all by yourself.

Ethical Decision-Making Strategies

Here are eight ethical decision-making strategies you can use when you have to decide what is the right thing to do. Think of it as your Ethics Toolbox. You can use these tools when you are unsure of the right thing to do.

GOLDEN RULE TEST. How would you feel if others did the same thing to you that you have done to them? If you would not want to have someone do the same thing to you, then the action is probably wrong.

TRUSTED ADULT TEST. What would your mom or dad, guardian, or other adult who is important in your life think? Your parents,

Gandhi Test

guardians, or other adults who are important to you may not understand the Internet, but they know a lot about deciding whether an action is right or wrong. Considering how your parents, guardians, or other important adult would judge your actions will help you to act in accordance with your family's values.

IS THERE A RULE? TEST. Generally, rules or laws have been created to protect the rights of people and serve the common good. Rules and laws provide good guidance on whether or not an action is right or wrong.

FRONT PAGE TEST. If your action were reported on the front page of the newspaper, what would other people think? One way to make good decisions is to act as if the whole world can see what you are doing.

IF EVERYBODY DID IT TEST. What would happen if everybody made a decision to do the same thing you do? Consider what kind of world this would be if everyone did what you are thinking of doing. You might think that you are only causing a little bit of harm. But if everyone else also did a little bit of harm, then someone else might suffer a lot of hurt.

REAL WORLD TEST. Would it be okay if you did this action or a similar action in the real world? Just because you do something in cyberspace does not mean that you cannot hurt someone. Actions in cyberspace can cause just as much harm to someone else as actions in the real world.

GANDHI TEST. Sometimes when people behave inappropriately on the Internet they claim that they are actually trying to make the

Internet a better place. Mahatma Gandhi was a great leader in India who led a successful revolution using nonviolent resistance. One of the things he said was: "We must be the change we wish to see." It is a good thing for people to try to make the Internet and the world a better place. But you will be most successful in making things better if you behave in a way that you want others to behave.

CHECK INSIDE TEST. How do you feel inside? We all have a "voice of conscience" inside of us that helps us figure out whether an action is right or wrong. If the inside of your body feels uncomfortable, the action is probably wrong. But if you have a feeling of peace and comfort inside, the action is probably right.

Rationalizations

Sometimes you might have an argument with yourself about whether an action is right or wrong. Part of you thinks that the action is probably wrong. But another part of you makes an argument that the action is okay.

What you may be doing is rationalizing. Many times people create rationalizations when they are trying to deny that they are doing something that they know deep down inside is wrong.

Here are some typical ways that people try to rationalize wrong behavior:

Finger of Blame: "He started it." "She asked for it."

Follow the Crowd: "Everybody does it."

If I Only Had a Brain: "He told me to do it."

No Harm: "I didn't really hurt anybody."

Little Bit: "It is only a little bit wrong."

Good Intentions: "I'm doing this for a good cause."

No Consequences: "Nobody ever gets caught."

New World: "Things have changed. What used to be considered wrong is now okay."

If you listen closely to the things other people say when they try to justify hurtful or wrong behavior online (and in the real world), you will probably find many of these kinds of rationalizations. You might also find yourself saying these kinds of things.

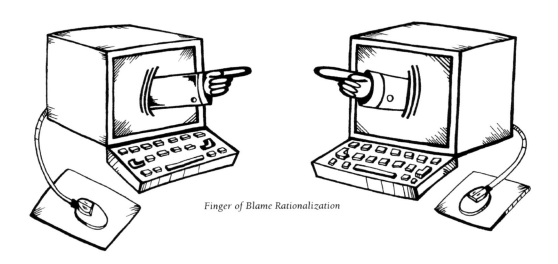

Finger of Blame Rationalization

For the Teacher

Activity 1

1. Have students write out on note cards three types of actions they think are irresponsible, unfair, unkind, or unsafe. Or have students use a word processor to do the same thing and print out their results.

2. Tape all the cards or printouts to a wall or chalkboard. Ask students to read all the cards. Encourage them to think about how the cards could be organized into groups.

3. Have students, as a class, devise a process by which they can categorize all the cards into groups of similar activities (e.g., hurtful speech, ignoring property rights).

4. Have students individually develop a set of rules that would prevent the kinds of actions described on the note cards.

5. Lead a discussion. Ask the students if the rules they devised reflect their personal values or simply practical necessity.

Activity 2

Have students write a short essay explaining how their lives would be different if they did have a ring that made them invisible. Make sure they address the following three questions:

1. What things would they be tempted to do, even if they knew it was wrong?

2. What positive or constructive actions could they take if they had such a ring?

3. What would be more important in regulating their actions—the chance that they might get caught and suffer the appropriate punishment, or their own moral and ethical values?

Activity 3

1. Give students a few minutes to brainstorm about times when they where forced to make a decision about the "rightness" or "wrongness" of an action. Have them write down at least three of the scenarios they remember.

2. Have the students go back and review the eight Ethical Decision-Making Strategies and pick three different "tests" they used or could have used in the situations they identified in Step 1. They should write out how applying the test helped or would have helped them make a decision.

Activity 4

1. Have students keep a "rationalizations log." Students should use the log to describe any occasion when they catch themselves using a rationalization to justify an action. In addition, they can keep track of other people using rationalizations to justify their behavior. (For privacy's sake, all entries should be anonymous).

2. Have students refer to the list of rationalizations provided in this unit. After each situation in their logs in which a rationalization was used, have them identify the type of rationalization that took place. For example, if some students note that they once surfed noneducational Web sites in the library because all their friends were doing it, they should note that they were using the Follow the Crowd Rationalization.

UNIT 2

Those Are Real People Out There

*A*my likes to go to an online gaming community chat room. However, each time she goes, the same person tries to isolate her for a personal chat. This person has been continually sending her personal e-mails. Amy has hinted that she does not wish to carry on a correspondence. Unfortunately, she can't seem to convey her discomfort. Why do you think this is so? What happens if you say something or do something to a friend that makes him or her sad, angry, or uncomfortable? How can you tell that you have caused harm to your friend?

Generally, it is pretty easy to figure this out. You can tell by the look on your friend's face or the sound of your friend's voice. But when you use the Internet, you cannot see or hear other people. Does this mean it is okay to say or do something that will hurt someone else?

Empathy

When you see or hear that your friend is sad, you feel sad. What causes you to feel sad is something called *empathy*. Empathy makes us feel bad if we hurt someone else. Empathy is a very important human trait that helps us to learn to avoid doing things that can hurt other people.

Empathy has two parts—a feeling part and a thinking part. When you see or hear someone who is happy or sad, you begin to feel the same way inside. This is the feeling part of empathy. As you grow, you also gain

No Harm Rationalization

the ability to understand how other people think and feel. You learn to think about things from another person's perspective. Thinking about how another person might feel can affect how you feel inside. This is the thinking part of empathy.

When you use the Internet, you might forget that your actions could hurt a real person. The reason you might forget is that you can't see or hear the other person, so the feeling part of empathy does not work. You have to rely on the thinking part of empathy. Think about how that unseen other person might feel as a result of your actions.

When you cannot see or hear other people, it is easier to use the No Harm Rationalization to convince yourself that you have not hurt them. Even though you know deep inside that your action was hurtful, it is easy to trick yourself into

believing that you have not done anything wrong because you cannot see or hear the other person.

Two of the Ethical Decision-Making Strategies are especially helpful in remembering that there are real people on the Internet who could be hurt by your actions. The strategies are the Real World Test (would I say or do this if the other person were sitting in front of me?) and the Golden Rule Test (how would I feel if someone said or did this to me?).

If you use these tests regularly, they will help you remember that there are real people out there.

What If Someone Hurts You?

Sometimes another person might not remember that you are a real person. Without realizing it, the other person might do or say something that hurts you. Be careful how you respond. You probably feel like trying to hurt the other person back. It is easy to rationalize attacking someone who has hurt you by using the Finger of Blame Rationalization. You can always claim that "he started it" or "she started it."

But hurting someone back will probably not help the other person realize that you were hurt. The other person will simply think that you are the "bad person" because you are the one who got angry and attacked. Your anger and attack will make it easier for the other person to ignore the fact that he or she did something that hurt you.

Remember, when it comes to the Internet, the other person might not recognize that he or she has hurt you. That person can't see or hear you. You can help this person recognize that what he or she did was not okay by communicating your feelings of hurt without attacking. If you do this, you will force the person to reflect on his or her own actions rather than blame you. Hopefully, this will help the other person understand how his or her actions have hurt you.

In cases like this, use the Golden Rule Test. If you forgot that someone was a real person and did something that hurt that person, would you want the person to try to hurt you back? Or would you want the person to tell you—in a way that will help resolve the problem—that what you did hurt.

A good way to communicate your feelings without attacking is to use "I" or "me" messages. Here are two examples: "I felt (describe your feelings) when you (describe his or her actions)" and "When you (describe his or her actions), it made me feel (describe your feelings)."

When you use "I" or "me" messages, you force the other person to recognize the hurt he or she has caused. This will help the other person learn not to do things that hurt.

The Internet can help to bring people in this world together. Hopefully, this will lead to greater peace and understanding in the world. But this will happen only if everybody remembers that there are real people out there. The way you treat people on the Internet who you cannot see or hear reflects on the kind of person you are.

Golden Rule Test

For the Teacher

Activity 1

As a class, have students offer examples of times when they were hurt or offended by an e-mail or chat room experience. Ask students how they responded to the situation.

As the teacher, assume the role of an anonymous character and send all your students a generic e-mail that shows a lack empathy. Have your students respond to the e-mail using the techniques described at the end of this unit. Make sure your students understand that you are role-playing and that the e-mail is fictitious.

Activity 2

The following simulation is designed to illustrate how anonymity and the inability to receive empathetic cues affect a person's ethical behavior.

1. Tell students that for participating in this assignment they will each receive 10 extra credit points in the grade book. However, at some point in the game, each student will have the opportunity to take a portion of another student's extra credit.

2. Assign each student a random number but do not tell the students what their individual numbers are.

3. Explain that, as the teacher, you will allow each student to take from 0 to 5 extra credit points from another student, but no student will know who that student is—each student will be known only as a number. (They should also be told that they will not be taking extra credit from themselves.) For example, go to the first student in class and say: "You may take from 0 to 5 extra credit points from student # _____."

4. After each student responds by indicating how many extra credit points he or she wants to take from another anonymous student, that amount should be added to the "taking" student's total of 10 and removed from the other student's total.

5. Half way through the activity, change the rules so that students know that they will be told which student they will be taking extra credit from. For example, you might say to a student: "You may take from 0 to 5 extra credit points from Johnny (or Sally)."

6. When every student has had a chance to participate, inform all students that they will each receive 10 extra credit points so that no one feels cheated.

7. Lead a discussion examining how the students' behavior changed when they were taking extra credit away from someone they knew.

UNIT 3

Play by the Rules

Max lost his computer privileges because he gave his personal password to a friend. Do you think this was fair? Think about how a community might function if there were no rules? What would it be like to live in a community where anyone could do anything he or she wanted, regardless of the problems this might cause to anyone else? Why do groups of people create rules? Is it okay to break a rule if you know that you will not be caught and punished?

Your school's Internet use policy has rules about how you can use the Internet at school. The policy contains two kinds of rules. Some rules are about safe and responsible online behavior. Other rules are about activities that are not appropriate when you use the Internet at school. These rules may or may not be important when you use the Internet at home or at a public location offering Internet access.

Rules for Safe and Responsible Online Behavior

Some of the rules in your school's Internet use policy are important because they will help you learn to use the Internet in a safe and responsible way. It is important to follow these rules whenever you use the Internet—at school or at home or at some other place where Internet access is provided. If you break these rules, you could hurt someone else or yourself.

Rules for safe and responsible online behavior are included in most school Internet use policies. Here are some typical types of rules covered. (Your school's specific policy may use different language, but the ideas and rules are likely to be similar.)

- Rules about actions that are illegal because they violate state or federal laws

- Rules about actions that are not safe or that may jeopardize your personal privacy

- Rules about actions that may jeopardize the safety and privacy of others

- Rules about actions that harm others or are disrespectful of others

- Rules about actions that can harm a computer system or disrupt the Internet

- Rules about actions that infringe the copyrights of others

- Rules about plagiarism

- Rules about accessing inappropriate material on the Internet

Rules for School Use of the Internet

Rules for school use define activities that are not appropriate in a school setting. The school Internet system is a specific-purpose Internet service. It was established for the specific purpose of supporting your education. Your school's Internet system is not to be used for playing games, shopping, or other activities that are not educational. It is not that these activities are wrong or harmful. They simply are not appropriate activities in a school setting. For example, kicking a soccer ball on a soccer field is perfectly okay, but kicking a soccer ball in your English class would not be okay.

A specific-purpose Internet system is different from a general-purpose Internet system. There are two basic kinds of general-purpose Internet systems. One is an Internet service provider that you access through your home computer. The other is a public access service

established by your public library or community technology center. Depending on the rules set by your parents and the public access service, activities like playing games and shopping may be acceptable on a general-purpose Internet system.

The Real World Test can help you figure out whether certain activities using the Internet are appropriate when you are at school. Think of a real-world activity that is similar to

Real World Test

the activity you want to do on the Internet. Then ask yourself, "Would it be okay to do this in the school library?" Here are some examples:

- **Is it okay to do your homework in the library?** Yes. The most important reason that your school provides Internet access is to support your schoolwork.

- **Is it okay to play video games in the library?** Probably not, unless you are playing an educational game. Playing games on the Internet is generally not okay in school. Your school may approve some educational games that are online.

- **Is it okay to read a newspaper or to look up information on a subject that you are**

not currently studying in class when you are in the library? Yes. It is okay for you to do research about things you are interested in. You do not have to restrict your research to your current schoolwork. Using the Internet to learn about an interesting topic is an important part of becoming a lifelong learner.

• **Is it okay to shop for a present for your mother in the library?** Probably not. Shopping online is not an educational activity.

• **Is it okay to look up information about possible college or career opportunities when you are in the library?** Of course it is. The same kinds of activities are okay on the Internet.

Some schools have established places and times, such as an open lab before and after school, when students can use the school Internet system for general-purpose activities. If you are using the school Internet system during an open-lab time, the rules for the kinds of activities that are appropriate may be different from the rules for your activities during school hours. It is important to remember that you must always follow the rules for safe and responsible online behavior.

When you get a job with a company, organization, or government agency, it will be important to remember the difference between a specific-purpose Internet system and a general-purpose Internet system. Internet systems established by companies, organizations, and government agencies are also specific-purpose Internet systems. As an employee, you will be required to restrict your use to those activities that support the business, organization, or agency. Having the self-control to use a specific-purpose Internet system only for its specific purpose is an important skill for success.

Your Parents' Rules

It is important to talk with your parents about their rules and expectations for your use of the Internet. Here are some issues you should talk about:

• When can you use the Internet?

• How much time should you spend using the Internet?

• What kinds of activities and Web sites do your parents approve of? What kinds of sites and activities do your parents not approve of?

• What kind of information about yourself is okay or not okay to disclose when you are using the Internet?

• What kind of information about your family is okay or not okay to disclose when you are using the Internet?

• What should you do if you become uncomfortable about something you find or someone who contacts you on the Internet?

It is also important to talk with your parents about their expectations for your use of the

Trusted Adult Test

Internet at school. Depending on your family's values, it may be that there are some sites the school thinks are okay for you to access but your parents don't agree. The school cannot enforce a wide range of family values, so you are encouraged to follow your individual family's values.

Use the Trusted Adult Test to make sure your use of the Internet is in accord with your family's values.

When Rules Are Not Right

There may be a time when you firmly believe that a rule that affects your use of the Internet is not right. This may be a school rule, a parent rule, or a rule at a public access site. It is not okay simply to violate a rule or a law because you think the rule is wrong. What you can do is responsibly challenge the rule or law. Here are some guidelines for responsibly challenging a rule that you think is not right:

- **Demonstrate respect for the people who created or are responsible for enforcing the rule.** It is okay to challenge a rule you

Is There a Rule? Test

believe is wrong, but it is not okay to treat other people disrespectfully. Remember that the rule has been established to address a problem.

- **Do your homework.** Before you challenge a rule, make sure that you have a solid, well-reasoned argument against the rule. You will need to know how and why the rule was created. There are several ways to make a well-reasoned argument against a rule. Demonstrate that the reason for the rule is not valid or that the problem the rule tries to address is not a valid problem. Demonstrate that the rule does not effectively address the problem it is supposed to address or that there are better ways to address the problem. Demonstrate that there are other issues of concern that make the rule unacceptable.

- **Present your position to the appropriate people, at the appropriate time and place.** If the problem is valid but the rule is not, propose a new rule that you think is more appropriate and will address the problem.

- **Carefully consider the arguments against your position.** Take the time to reanalyze your position before you respond.

- **If you continue to think that you are in the right, hold to your position.** Continue to raise your arguments to the appropriate people, in the appropriate time and place.

- **If your arguments are unsuccessful in getting the rule changed, accept defeat graciously and respectfully.** Look for other opportunities to challenge the rule. Sometimes change takes time.

If you choose to challenge a rule you think is not right, it is very important to follow the Gandhi Test. The only effective way to create positive change is to maintain high ethical standards for your own behavior.

For the Teacher

Activity 1

Your students have just been magically transported to an uninhabited island. There are no adults, no police, and no game show hosts. There are no rules (other than the rules of nature). Discuss the possible outcomes. Would your students decide that it was necessary to create some basic rules? If not, how do they think their group would function? If they did decide to create rules, what basic rules would they create? This activity could be done as a discussion, role-playing session, or essay.

Activity 2

1. The day before using this lesson, have students sit down with a parent or guardian and establish or review their expectations or rules for home-based Internet use. If students do not have a computer at home, have them and their parents or guardians establish rules for the use of a friend's computer or a computer in the public library.

2. In class the next day, hand out a copy of the school's Internet use policy. Discuss the similarities and differences between the school's rules and the students' parental rules.

3. You may want to have students develop a list of rules that should be—but are not— among the school and parental rules. You might also have students develop a list of rules that should be eliminated. Be prepared to discuss rules that they feel should be removed.

Activity 3

Ask students to identify a rule or law they do not agree with. This rule can be either a state or federal law, a school rule, or a parental rule. Have students write, either individually or in teams, a Letter to the Editor (a maximum of 300 words) explaining their rationale for why the rule or law is inappropriate and how it should be changed.

Activity 4

Pose the following question to your students: Why it is okay to break a rule when using the Internet if I know I will not get caught and punished? Ask them to brainstorm a list of reasons why it might be okay. (If this is difficult for them, ask them to consider arguments they might have heard other students make when rationalizing why this might be okay.) After the class has created the list of reasons, have students compare the reasons with the rationalizations provided in the Unit 1, "What You Do Reflects on You."

Now, change the question: Why it is not okay to break a rule when using the Internet, even though I know I will not get caught and punished? Have students brainstorm why it might not be okay to break a rule. Develop a concise list of the reasons and post it in the classroom.

UNIT 4

Keep It Private

Amy is upset about a relationship with a close friend. She writes an e-mail message to another friend describing what is happening. She shares intimate details about personal activities involving the close friend and information about problems the friend is having with parents. The person Amy sent this message to forwards the message to several other people. How do you think Amy is going to feel when she finds out? How would you feel if someone did this to you?

It is important to learn to protect your own privacy and respect the privacy of others when you use the Internet. Because you can feel invisible when you use the Internet, you might not think about how other people may be able to use your personal information. But the Internet is never private. It is very important that you always remember that everything you do or write when using the Internet is stored in electronic form someplace. Others may be able to track or access what you have done or what you have said.

The level of privacy you can expect when you use the Internet can vary from place to place, just like in the real world. It is not a very good idea to talk about private matters in the middle of the school cafeteria. The important lesson to learn is where you can expect to have some privacy on the Internet and where you cannot expect to have any privacy. Then you must guide your behavior accordingly.

Protecting Your Own Privacy

Have you ever kept a diary or journal? The kinds of things you write in a diary or journal are very personal and private. Sometimes when you are using the Internet, it can feel as if you are writing in a diary or personal journal. But it is not. Whatever you do on the Internet is recorded on a computer somewhere. Other people can learn things about you that you might not want them to know.

It is very important that you think about privacy whenever you use the Internet. There are many ways your privacy can be invaded. Most of what you do on the Internet is not private.

It is important for you to think about the kinds of information about you that you want to keep private. It is also important for you to talk with your parents about the kinds of information about your family that should be kept private. When you

Front Page Test

use the Internet, be careful about disclosing any information that you or your family might want to keep private.

Use the Front Page Test. Would you want the information you are thinking of disclosing to appear on the front page of a newspaper?

Respecting the Privacy of Others

It is not okay to share private information about other people in public or private electronic messages or anyplace else on the Internet. This includes private information about other people in your family. The personal information of other people is their private business. Only they have the right to choose to disclose this information. Once you have sent a message, you have no control over where that message might travel. You may be responsible for sharing information that could really hurt another person.

What people say in private messages to you should be treated with respect. If someone sends you an e-mail message, you should not forward the message to someone else without getting permission from the person who sent it to you.

Use the Golden Rule Test. Would you want your friends to share your personal information or forward your personal messages without your permission?

Privacy on a School Account

You should not expect to have privacy when you use the Internet at school. Your school must make sure that students use the Internet and school computers appropriately. All student use of the Internet is, and must be, supervised and monitored

Trusted Adult Test

Schools have different policies for e-mail accounts and student privacy. Some schools allow no individual e-mail accounts. Other schools allow individual e-mail accounts but make it clear that teachers and administrators can look at student e-mail files at any time and for any reason. Other schools tell students that they have a limited expectation of privacy in their e-mail. At these schools, administrators will look at student e-mail files only if there is a reasonable expectation that the student has used the Internet in a way that violates a school rule or the law. This rule is similar to the rule administrators use for individual searches of student lockers or desks. Schools will always allow your parents to have access to your e-mail files.

by the school. Your parents also have the right to access your files on the school computer system.

Your school monitors all Web activity. There are two reasons for this. One is concern about student access to Web sites that are not appropriate. The second is that the school is looking at student use of the Internet to determine how it can be used most effectively to support education.

The URL for each site you visit is recorded on the system server. The school can print out a list of all the Web sites accessed through your account. Some schools have technical monitoring systems that allow the teacher or computer lab monitor to see what all students are doing at their computers. Teachers and lab monitors are also responsible for watching students when they are using the Internet.

When you graduate and get a job, you may have Internet access through your employer. The only reason employers provide Internet access is to support the activities of the business or agency. Your Internet account on an employer system is not a private personal account. Many employers regularly monitor the activities of employees when they are using the Internet. As you learn to monitor your activities on the school account, you will gain skills that will help you in the future.

The Front Page Test or the Trusted Adult Test are very good to consider whenever you use the Internet on a school account. Remember at all times that whatever you do can be monitored and reviewed by the school and by your parents. A variation of the Real World Test can also be a helpful guide. Would you do what you are thinking of doing in the middle of your real-world school cafeteria?

Protecting Your Privacy in Discussion Groups and Chat Rooms

Be especially careful about sharing personal information in a message that is sent to an online discussion group, such as a newsgroup or mailing list. Many discussion-group messages are archived on a computer system somewhere. They are easily accessible by anyone who knows how to search for them. You should think about what might happen if your personal information could be found by anyone who wanted to see it at any time in the future.

One of the nice things about the Internet is that you can join online communities and discuss personal concerns with others who share those same concerns. Because of the limited privacy you have on a school Internet system, engaging in sensitive online group discussions through a school account is not recommended. One option is to use the public access Internet service at your public library or community technology center. If you participate in a discussion group that is discussing sensitive issues, you can also establish an anonymous e-mail account through a Web-based e-mail service. In this way, your messages are much less likely to be traced back to you. However, it is never appropriate to use an anonymous e-mail account to cause harm or to send messages that include hurtful language. Even anonymous e-mail accounts are not truly anonymous. The company providing the service can identify users. If you hurt someone through an anonymous account, your identity can be discovered.

Make sure you use the Check Inside Test before revealing any personal information in a discussion group or chat room. Are you really comfortable knowing that the information you are about to reveal will be stored someplace for someone else to find and read?

Protecting Your Privacy on Commercial Sites

Generally, it is not appropriate for you to access sites that sell products or have a substantial amount of banner advertising when you are using the Internet at school. However, there may be times when you need to access such sites for a class assignment. You may also access these commercial sites from your home computer or through the library or community technology center.

Commercial Web sites are very interested in obtaining as much personal information from you as they can. Sometimes they use this information to provide you with specific content on their site. But mostly they are interested in

Real World Test

finding out as much as they can about you so that they can deliver specific banner ads that display products or services you will be interested in. Their goal is financial. They want you to spend your money, or convince your parents to spend money, on the products or services that are advertised.

Online Profiling

What these Web sites are doing is called *online profiling*. A computer collects large amounts of information from and about you, which is stored, analyzed, and then used to make decisions about the kinds of banner ads to present to you when you are on a given Web site. Presenting specific banner advertisements to you is called *targeted advertising*.

Here is how profiling and targeted advertising work. A Web site, or the company that provides banner ads on the Web site, may have found out that you are really interested in sports. You may have told them this information or they may have figured it out because you are always visiting sports Web sites. Now, whenever you go to a Web site associated with the banner ad company, you will be presented with banner ads for sporting goods and other products that people interested in sports tend to be interested in. The Web site knows you are interested in sports and thinks you will be more likely to click on banner ads for sports items. The Web site makes money when you click on the ads.

Most Web sites explain the kinds of information they are collecting and what they intend to do with the information in a document called a *privacy policy*. If you are under the age of 13 and the company is collecting personal information from you, the company must follow the provisions of

the Children's Online Privacy Protection Act (COPPA). COPPA is a federal law that was enacted in an attempt to prevent companies from taking advantage of younger children.

Unfortunately, many privacy policies are written using language that is hard to understand. On other occasions, companies may use language that attempts to make you think that what they are doing is really nice and helpful for you. For example, a privacy policy may state, "We collect information about your interests so that we can provide you with advertising experiences that are appropriate." What the company is really saying is, "We want to find out as much about you as we can so that we can use this information to try to convince you to click on certain ads and buy certain products or services."

Companies collect information both directly and indirectly. To collect information directly requires your participation. You must be willing to provide personal information on the Web site. You might not be aware that your personal information could be stored for years in a computer database. The primary ways companies collect information directly are through registration forms, surveys, polls, questionnaires, and contests. It is important to recognize the companies' motives and their techniques and to make your own decisions about how much personal information you are willing to reveal.

Companies also collect information from you indirectly. They do this by placing a tiny bit of computer data, called a *cookie*, on your personal computer. This cookie can then report back to the Web site that placed it where you go and what you do on the Internet. If you use the Internet at home you can set your Internet browser to either reject the placement of cookies or to notify you and request permission prior to allowing a Web site to place a cookie.

To learn more about how to block cookies go to www.junkbusters.com.

What You Can Do

There are some very practical steps you can take to protect your privacy on commercial sites.

- **Talk with your parents about the kinds of information about you and about your family you may disclose on the Internet.**

- **When you visit a new Web site, read the privacy policy.** Then look around a bit to see if this site really is of interest to you. If the site requires you to register, ask yourself whether you are interested enough in what the site has to offer to give up your personal privacy. If you choose to register, fill in only those parts of the form that are required for registration. Check with your parents before providing any personal contact information on a Web site.

- **When you are on a commercial Web site, be careful about responding to any questionnaires, surveys, or polls, or entering any contests.** Many of these are just gimmicks to try to trick you into providing personal information. Protecting your privacy might be more important than the chance to win some prize.

New systems are under development that will allow you, in the future, to have greater control over your personal private information. Even when these systems become available, you will remain the most important guardian of your personal information. Use the Check Inside Test before you provide any information on a commercial Web site. Do you want the information the Web site requests from you to be kept in a computer database and used in ways that you will have no control over for years into the future?

Check Inside Test

For the Teacher

Activity 1

Invite the school or district technology director to your class to discuss how the district tracks and analyzes student use of the Internet. Provide students with sample logs that track student activity.

Activity 2

1. Send your students on an online scavenger hunt. Each student or student team should find one example of the following:

   a. A gift or contest entry that seeks disclosure of personal information.

   b. A site that seeks disclosure of personal contact information about a friend.

   c. A site that seeks personal information about family members.

   d. A teen poll or survey that seeks personal information.

   e. A statement on a Web site informing the student that failure to provide personal information will result in an inability to access the Web site.

   f. Any other invasion of privacy. (Students should find as many examples as they can.)

   g. The most confusing provision in a privacy policy.

2. After the scavenger hunt is over, students should present to the entire class examples of what they found and vote on what they feel is the most invasive example.

Activity 3

Make a master list of all the kinds of personal information students have been requested to provide on commercial Web sites. Instruct your students to take the list home and have a conversation with their parents about online privacy. The students and their parents should review the list and place the items into three categories: (1) okay to reveal, (2) check with parents, (3) never okay to reveal.

Activity 4

The Web page on the Responsible Netizen Web site (www.netizen.uoregon.edu) established to support this book provides links to current news stories regarding privacy issues that can be used instructionally in various ways. Have students pick an Internet privacy issue and write an essay or opinion piece on it. Or have students collaboratively create a news broadcast on current online privacy issues.

UNIT 5

Look Your Best

Max is very interested in astronomy. He finds an e-mail discussion group about astronomy that includes other teens and adults who have interests in astronomy, including university faculty and researchers. Max posts regularly to the site and pays close attention to the content and appearance of the messages he submits to the group. One day, Max receives an offer of a scholarship to attend a four-week astronomy workshop at a nearby university. The professor making the offer indicates that the knowledge and interest Max demonstrated has been very impressive. What do you think Max did to impress the professor?

Are you the kind of person who cares about what other people think of you? Do you want other people to respect your opinions and ideas? Or is it okay with you that other people simply delete your messages because they think you have nothing important to say?

When you communicate with other people on the Internet, nobody can see what you look like. Other people can't tell your age, your race, or even if you are having a bad hair day. They will form an impression about you based only on how you "appear" in your online writings. How do your electronic messages reflect on you?

When you use the Internet at school, you are expected to communicate in a way that reflects positively on you and your school. One of the reasons the school has established Internet access is to help you learn the skills to effectively communicate online.

You may be surprised at the possible benefits if you look your best when you write online. Some young people have been offered exciting educational and job opportunities because they impressed others in their online communications. Here are some guidelines for looking your best online:

Golden Rule Test

- **Think about who you are writing to and write in a style that is appropriate.** If you wrote a note to a friend, what would it look like? How would this note be different from a note you might write to your principal? Some messages should be written in a casual style. Other

messages should be written more formally. Whenever you communicate electronically through the school's Internet system to an adult or someone you do not know, you should use a more formal style.

- **Make sure you have addressed your message properly.** It is embarrassing to send a message to the wrong person. If you send a message to the wrong address you may disclose private information to someone who should not receive that information. Be very careful if you are trying to respond privately to a message you have received through a group discussion. If you are not careful, your private message may be sent to the entire group.

- **Use a subject heading that describes what your message is about.** This will capture the attention of the person or people receiving your message.

- **Take the time to proofread your message.** Check your spelling, grammar, and punctuation.

- **People tend to read electronic messages quickly.** You can help them read your message easily. Make sure your topic sentence is the first sentence in the paragraph. Keep your paragraphs short and to the point. Include a blank line between each paragraph.

- **Make sure your message is clear and logical.** Don't be long-winded. Short messages that focus on one topic are much better than long messages that cover different topics.

- **Always identify who you are—but only to the extent that is permitted by your school or your parents.** When you communicate through your school account, provide only the amount of personal information that is allowable

Front Page Test

- **Be careful when you use sarcasm or humor.** Other people can't see your face, so it is hard for them to figure out whether you are joking or are serious. Other people may become hurt or angry if they do not recognize that you are simply trying to be funny.

A variation of the Front Page Test is good to use when you are writing a message. Consider the impression your message would make if it were printed in the Letters to the Editor section of a newspaper. Just remember, whatever you write reflects on you. Other people will judge you solely on your writing.

through your school account. When you communicate from home, provide only the personal information that your parents have approved.

- **When you are communicating in a group discussion, make sure you stick to the group's topic.** Most group members will not be interested in your views on other issues.

- **Add some color to your messages.** The use of *asterisks* to emphasize a point or the use of a smiley :-) to provide an illustration of what you are feeling can make your message more interesting to read. You can also emphasize key points by using bullets or different fonts or colors. But don't overdo it, and PLEASE AVOID SHOUTING! (If you use all capital letters, people will think you are shouting.)

"What you do reflects on you"

For the Teacher

Activity 1

1. Have students write an e-mail to a fictitious principal, breaking as many rules as possible for "looking your best."

2. Have students print out the e-mail and exchange it with a partner.

3. Have the partners identify all the intentional errors and then rewrite the message in acceptable form.

4. Have the partners meet to make sure they found all the mistakes included in the original e-mail.

Activity 2

Prior to the class, find some e-mail messages that demonstrate positive and negative examples of the "looking your best" guidelines. All identifying information should be stripped from the messages. Give your students the messages and ask them to identify places where the guidelines have been followed and places where the guidelines have not been followed. Ask them to rewrite sections of the e-mail messages where the guidelines were not followed.

UNIT 6

Don't Pollute

*A*my *thinks the school debate teacher insults the students during his lectures. To respond, she creates a Web site about the debate teacher. The Web site contains crude pictures and unflattering stories about the debate teacher. Students are invited to submit descriptions, stories, or comments about the teacher, which are posted on the Web site. Would you log on to the site? What if someone created a Web site about you?*

Are you the kind of person who thinks that when you communicate or post material on the Internet, you have the freedom of speech to say anything you want—even though what you say might cause harm to someone else?

Regardless of whether or not you have the right to communicate something, it is also important to consider the harm you may cause to others by doing so. Most democratic governments in the world grant the right of free speech to their citizens. The right to speak freely is considered essential to our democracy.

This right ensures that the government cannot suppress unpopular ideas.

But the right of free speech is not absolute. You do not, for example, have the right to yell "Fire!" in a crowded theater. And just because you may have the right to say something does not mean that you cannot be held responsible for the harm caused by what you say. Sometimes, inappropriate speech can cause so much harm to someone else that you (and your parents) can be sued in court for the damage caused by the speech. Some inappropriate speech is considered to be against the law.

Your school has an obligation to make sure that all students and staff feel welcomed and comfortable in the school environment. The school has the right to discipline students for speech that is inappropriate or causes harm. When you use the Internet at school, any form of inappropriate or harmful speech is considered a violation of the Internet use policy, as well as other disciplinary rules. It is also important to consider how your communication on the Internet outside of school may affect others within your school.

Good Intentions Rationalization

Here are some guidelines to follow:

- **Be polite.** Do not use obscene, profane, lewd, vulgar, rude, inflammatory, threatening, or disrespectful language. Remember, other people will judge you based on the language you use.

- **Treat others with respect.** Do not engage in personal attacks. If you attack someone else, it says much more about the kind of person you are than it does about the person you attack.

- **If it isn't true, don't say it.** Do not make a false public statement about a person or company. This is considered defamation. You or your parents can be held liable in a civil lawsuit for damages if you make a false public statement that causes injury to someone's reputation.

- **If you are ever told by someone to stop sending him or her messages, stop.** If the person receiving your messages does not want to receive your messages and has told you so, continuing to send messages is considered harassment.

People who "pollute" the Internet generally try to rationalize their online pollution. If they use profane or obscene language, they will claim that "everyone does it" (using the Follow the Crowd Rationalization).

If the polluter has hurt someone by engaging in personal attacks, defamation, or harassment, the polluter will try to point the finger of blame at the person who was hurt (using the Finger of Blame Rationalization), will try to blame someone else (using the If I Only Had a Brain Rationalization), or will claim that the pollution was for a good cause (using the Good Intentions Rationalization).

Several ethical decision-making strategies are good for assessing whether you should send a person a message:

- **Use the Golden Rule Test for your communications on the Internet.** How would you feel if someone wrote the same or a similar thing to you or about you that you are writing to another person?

- **Use the If Everybody Did It Test.** Would you like using the Internet if everyone were polluting it?

- **Use the Real World Test.** Pollution is not okay in the real world, and it is not okay on the Internet.

Sometimes young people use the Internet to express angry thoughts when it seems as if there is no other way to communicate those thoughts. You may have a perfect right to be angry. You may be the victim of bullying or harassment. Other people may not be treating you with respect or kindness.

The problem with using the Internet to express your anger is that it will look to others as if you are the one who is causing the problem. People will think badly of you. And you are the one who will get into trouble. If you are being bullied or harassed, don't take your anger to the Internet. This will only make things worse. Talk with your parents, a teacher, a counselor, or a trusted friend. Tell them about how others are treating you and how you are feeling.

At other times young people may use the Internet to protest the actions of other people. They may post a site that protests the actions of a person, a teacher, a principal, companies, elected officials, government agencies, or others. Using the Internet to communicate concerns about the actions of others is perfectly okay. Students have a free-speech right to publish materials that express disagreement and disapproval of the actions of others. But engaging in online pollution is not okay. Effective online protesters focus on the facts and provide reasoned arguments to protest the actions of others. People who use online pollution to protest the actions of others are not successful in creating positive change. They merely create lots of hurt and make lots of people mad at them. If you want to create a Web site to protest something or challenge rules that are not right, follow the guidelines in Unit 3, "Play by the Rules."

If Everybody Did It Test

For the Teacher

Activity 1

In an essay or class debate, have students address the question of how a school administrator should respond to Amy's Web site described in the scenario at the beginning of this unit.

Activity 2

1. Have students find some advocacy groups that are effectively using the Internet to communicate their concerns.

2. Have students evaluate the effectiveness of the actions of online advocacy groups. What are the common characteristics of effective online advocacy groups?

UNIT 7

Remain Cool under Fire

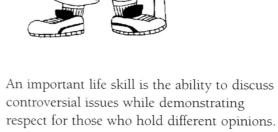

Max is participating in a teen discussion list. Another participant just wrote a message criticizing students who have pierced body parts and tattoos. Max is very angry and responds to the message using profane language and accusing the other participant of being a racist. Do you think the argument is going to end there or escalate? What could have Max done better?

People do not always agree about things. Unfortunately, when people communicating on the Internet disagree, it can sometimes lead to what are called *flame wars*. Flame wars are online written fights.

Flame wars are sometimes started by people who are just plain rude and want to get into online fights. On other occasions, a flame war may start when one person unintentionally hurts another person or makes another person mad. The person who was hurt or got upset responds by attacking the first person. The first person then attacks back and other people jump into the fight.

You have the right to express your views on a matter, even if your views are controversial.

An important life skill is the ability to discuss controversial issues while demonstrating respect for those who hold different opinions.

Here are some tips for how to remain cool under fire when online controversy erupts:

- **Never respond to flame bait.** Flame bait is a message posted by a rude and obnoxious person with the intention of starting a flame war.

- **If someone has said something stupid or annoying, it is generally best to just ignore the message.** Other people in the group will form their own impressions about the person who wrote the message.

- **Challenge ideas or statements you find unacceptable but make it clear that you are not intending to personally attack other people.**

- **Explain why you feel so strongly about a particular issue.** By letting people know why you feel strongly about the issue, you help make it clear that your concern is the issue, not a desire to personally attack people who think otherwise.

- **If you want to express a strong opinion on an issue, write a short, clear message that presents a logical analysis of your opinion.** Provide a follow-up message or two that further explains your position or responds to a question. Then

stop. You cannot win in an online disagreement. The best you can do is help other people think about the issue from a new perspective.

- **Slow down!** If someone has said something that makes you mad, do not respond immediately. People who respond immediately to a message that has made them mad almost always regret what they have done—shortly after they press the Send button. You may write a response while you are still mad, but do not send it. Put your response into your Drafts folder. Then go back and reread your response after you have cooled down. With a cool head, you can send the message, rewrite the message, or trash the message.

- **Recognize that people have different opinions and have a right to have different opinions.** A person may state

Follow the Crowd Rationalization

People who frequently flame on the Internet use many of the same rationalizations as online polluters. Flamers will claim that "everyone does it" (using the Follow the Crowd Rationalization), will try to point the finger of blame at the person who was flamed (using the Finger of Blame Rationalization), will try to blame someone else (using the If I Only Had a Brain Rationalization), or will claim that the flaming was for a good cause (using the Good Intentions Rationalization).

Use the Golden Rule Test or Real World Test when you communicate on the Internet, especially if you are angry. How do you want people to treat you in the real world if they disagree with you or if something you have said or done has made them angry? Does it make you feel good to have people yell at you, or call you names, or put you down? Probably not. Probably you want others to treat you with respect, even if they disagree with you.

Real World Test

his or her opinion in a very irritating or even hurtful way. But if you personally attack that person for his or her opinion, you are the one who will have done the greater amount of damage.

- **If you are personally attacked online, you are in a position to win or lose—and it is your call.** If you respond in anger, you will lose. If you respond calmly and explain your position without attacking the other person, you will be viewed as the more responsible person.

- **If you find that people often appear to attack you, look closely at your messages.** You may be expressing your ideas in a way that hurts other people's feelings. Even if you are not intending to attack, your messages may be making other people think they are being attacked.

- **If you lose your temper and send a "flaming" message, acknowledge your mistake and apologize as soon as possible.**

Golden Rule Test

For the Teacher

Activity 1

1. Assign each student a partner. Have the first student write an e-mail to his or her partner expressing views on a subject he or she feels very passionately about (e.g., free speech, the death penalty, gender equality).

2. Ask the second student to play "devil's advocate" and return the e-mail, disagreeing with many of the points the partner has made. You may even want to encourage the student to goad the partner by making outrageous counter arguments.

3. Have the original e-mailer draft a logical response, avoiding all of the potential pitfalls described in this unit.

4. If time permits, have the two students reverse roles.

5. When the assignment is completed, lead a class discussion. Ask students (a) how they initially wanted to respond to the e-mails and (b) why they think a calmer response is better in the long run.

Activity 2

1. Have students log on to a live chat or discussion about current political issues. These chat rooms can be found on most newspaper or television Web sites (nytimes.com or msnbc.com). Students can watch or practice participating in highly charged discussions while "remaining cool under fire."

2. If a flame war erupts, have students analyze the messages related to the flame war. Pay special attention to the messages that preceded a flaming message.

UNIT 8

Read with Your Eyes Open

Amy is writing a report for science class. She finds some articles on a personal Web site hosted on a free Web site service. The author of the articles claims to have a Ph.D. and to be an internationally recognized authority on the subject. Should Amy try to verify the truth of this claim? How would she do it?

There is an incredible amount of information on the Internet. Some information is true and accurate. Some information is false or highly biased. Some information presents opinions that may or may not be based on accurate facts. Some information is designed to encourage you to adopt certain attitudes, which may or may not be healthy attitudes.

Normally, the information you receive in school is relatively accurate and unbiased. Textbook and library book publishers, teachers, and librarians all help screen the information students receive for accuracy and appropriateness. But sometimes even these educational materials present biased or incomplete information.

When you access material through the Internet, it may or may not have been carefully screened. An important life skill in the Information Age is the ability to determine what information is accurate and what information is not accurate. You will be able to practice this skill when you use the Internet in school.

Here are some guidelines for evaluating information found on the Internet:

- **Start with the recognition that there are no Cyberspace Truth Monitors.** There is no person, company, or government agency making sure that what people tell you or the information you find on a Web site is accurate and unbiased. You will need to be your own judge. While you are in school, your teachers and librarians will help you learn to determine whether information is accurate and unbiased.

- **Consider the source of the information.** Is the information provided by a university, government agency, or well-respected organization with expertise in the subject? If you have received a response to a question you have posted, who is the response from and what is the person's apparent background or expertise?

- **Look for evidence of bias.** Does the material appear to be presented for the purpose of providing information? Or is the material presented to persuade you to agree with a position taken by the person or organization providing the information? There is a higher probability that material presented by an advocacy organization to persuade you to take a certain position is more biased. This does not mean that the information presented is not accurate. It means that you have to be more careful in your evaluation of the information.

- **Determine whether the information is consistent with information found through other sources.** Is the same information present at several locations? Have you received several consistent responses to your question? Or is the information you have found conflicting?

- **Consider how you found the information.** Did you find the information by following a link from a recognized high-quality information resource, such as a library home page or an educational resource list? Information you find through a direct link from a library or education information resource is more likely to have been screened for accuracy.

- **Ask for the opinions of others, especially your teacher or librarian.** What do they think of the document or response to a question? What do they think of the source?

- **Evaluate the information itself. Is it logical?** Is it consistent with what you already know to be true? Does it "feel" right?

If you pay attention to the guidelines given in this unit, you will be able to develop a more sensitive Check Inside Test. Look carefully at the clues. Then check inside to determine whether or not you can trust the information you have found.

Check Inside Test

For the Teacher

Activity 1

1. Have students create a list of three possible research topics. (You can also let them use a research topic they are already working on.)

2. Have students search the Internet, looking for three resources for their research topics that would meet appropriate academic standards. They should identify what evidence they found that indicates the reference meets academic standards.

3. Have students find three resources that do not meet academic standards and again indicate what evidence they found to suggest this.

Activity 2

• Students need to be able to distinguish between opinions and facts on the Internet. To practice this skill development, have students search the Web on a controversial topic of their choice. You may need to help some students find an appropriate controversial topic.

• Once they have selected their topics, have them do some research on the Web about their topic. Have students track where they went to find information on their topic (Web site names and URLs), recording the information on a piece of paper or with a word processor. They should also provide a brief summary of the information they found.

• Next, have them attempt to determine if the information they found on the Web sites is opinion, fact, or a little of both. They may have to cross-reference the information they find with other sources (e.g., books, encyclopedias, periodicals) in order to accomplish this task.

• Once the students have completed their projects, have them compile the results. How many Web sites contained opinions or simple inaccuracies?

UNIT 9

Credit the Source

*M*ax has fallen behind in his homework. He has a research paper about the conflict in the Middle East due tomorrow for world history class. Max searches the Web for research resources and finds two papers written by other students on the same subject. He copies major sections from these two papers to create a research paper for class. What would you do if you were in the same situation? What were Max's other options?

Plagiarism means taking ideas or writings from another person and offering them as your own. Plagiarism has always been considered wrong. Computers and the Internet just make it easier to plagiarize. Computers allow you to "cut and paste" ideas and writings of other people into your own paper. It is also very easy to find research papers written by other people on Web sites.

Plagiarism is considered cheating and is a violation of school rules. The reason you are

required to conduct research and write papers in school is that these skills are important for your continuing success in education. For many of you, these skills will also be very important for your career.

There are two kinds of plagiarism: intentional and inadvertent.

INTENTIONAL PLAGIARISM. You intentionally plagiarize if you turn in a paper that was written by someone else and you represent it as your own work. You are also intentionally plagiarizing if you copy portions from someone else's paper into your paper, even if the portions are as small as a sentence or paragraph.

There are several ways that students use the Internet to find papers that they can intentionally plagiarize. One way is to find a Web site that sells or provides research papers specifically for students to copy and submit as their own. Another way is to find papers that other students have written and posted on the Internet.

Teachers know about this kind of plagiarism and look closely at the papers they receive for evidence of intentional plagiarism. Many times teachers can use search engines to find the original works. Teachers also can recognize when a student turns in a paper not written in the student's usual writing style.

There are several reasons why students might intentionally plagiarize. Some students do not

Little Bit Rationalization

think that they can write well but want to get a good grade. If you think that you have problems with writing, you should talk to a teacher or a counselor and find out how you can improve your skills. Your teachers want to make sure that all their students become good writers and will provide you with help and support. There also are Web sites that can help you with suggestions on how to write good papers.

Other students intentionally plagiarize because they did not plan their study schedule well and waited until the last minute to do their assignment. If you have just one night to complete a major paper and have not started, there is a strong temptation to plagiarize. If you have "blown it" and cannot turn in a paper when it is due, talk to your teacher or a counselor. It will be far better for you to take an "Incomplete" and turn in your work at a later date than to plagiarize.

Students who intentionally plagiarize may use a variety of rationalizations. They may try to rationalize that it is okay to plagiarize because everyone else does (the Follow the Crowd Rationalization). Or they may rationalize that that it is only a little bit wrong (the Little Bit Rationalization), and they won't get caught (the No Consequences Rationalization). Students may also rationalize that getting a good grade (the Good Intentions Rationalization) is more important than doing the work themselves.

Use the Check Inside Test or Front Page Test when you are in doubt about what to do. When you plagiarize on purpose, you are really cheating yourself. Successful people know how to accomplish their work without using unfair shortcuts. Cheating may provide a temporary reward of getting a good grade. But people who think it is okay to cheat always have to worry about the time when someone finds out that they have cheated.

INADVERTENT PLAGIARISM. This kind of plagiarism is more accidental. Students sometimes inadvertently plagiarize because they do not understand how to appropriately use the information written by others in their own papers, or they may not know how to properly cite their references.

When you write a kind of a paper called an essay, it will primarily contain your own thoughts. But when you write a research paper, you are expected to include the thoughts and ideas of other writers. When you include another writer's idea in your paper, you must give credit to the person whose idea you have used. You do so by using a proper citation. If you use the actual words written by another person, you must enclose the words in quotation marks and use a proper citation.

Here are some ways to avoid inadvertent plagiarism:

- **Keep track of your references.** When you take notes from other books, papers, or articles, copy all of the necessary bibliographic information for your reference. Such information usually includes the author, title, publication, and date of publication. When you find information on the Internet, you will need to have the URL. It is helpful to keep a separate document that contains your bibliography list. In this document you should routinely record the complete bibliographic citation for every document you read. Then, in your notes, you can briefly reference the source and the page number.

- **Keep your notes in a uniform manner.** You can use note cards or an electronic outliner. When you make notes, keep track of four categories of information:

1. Your own thoughts

2. Information that is general or common knowledge.

3. Your own summary or paraphrase of someone else's ideas and the source of these ideas.

4. Direct quotations from other documents and the source of these quotations.

- **When you download or copy material from the Internet, make sure you keep track of the URL and any other reference information.** When you are surfing the Web, it is very easy to become focused on the information you are finding and forget to record the source of the information.

- **If you use a direct quotation, make sure you:**

1. Quote accurately. You should not paraphrase a quotation.

2. Fit the quotation into your own text in a logical manner.

3. Use quotation marks.

4. Indent the quotation if it is long, usually over four lines.

5. Cite the reference properly.

- **If you paraphrase or summarize material, make sure you:**

1. Restate the ideas in your own words. Simple word changes are not acceptable.

2. Enclose any key words or phrases in quotes.

3. Cite the reference properly.

- **If you include your own thoughts or information that is common knowledge, there is no need for a citation.** But ask your teacher for advice if you are unsure whether or not the information is common knowledge.

For the Teacher

Activity 1

In Unit 8, "Read with Your Eyes Open," students identified three sources and references for a research project. For this assignment, they will use those three sources.

1. Have students log on to the Web site www.apastyle.org/elecref.html, which deals with electronic citation issues. Have them read the section at this site titled "Reference Examples for Electronic Source Materials."

2. When they have finished, have them use the information they have learned to draft sample citations for the references they found in the previous assignment.

Activity 2

Have the students brainstorm reasons or factors they think might cause a student to engage in plagiarism. For each reason or factor, discuss a strategy that could be used to prevent plagiarism.

Activity 3

Have the students look at the Web sites of universities and colleges in your region to find these schools' policies on plagiarism. Discuss the common provisions.

UNIT 10

Respect the Creator

Amy just purchased a new computer and has borrowed a friend's word-processing, spreadsheet, and database software programs. She installs these programs on her new computer. Even though this violates federal law, do you think she has done anything wrong? What if you had written the programs she copied?

Copyright laws balance two important values. First, they protect the rights of the creator, who has created something of value and should have the right to say who can use it and how. Second, they provide benefits to society by making sure that people can receive income from their creative efforts. We encourage people to create, and we all benefit from their creations.

Your Copyright Rights

Why is it important for young people to learn about copyright law? The most important reason is that copyright law gives you the right to protect any work you create, whether in school or at home. The Internet provides you with the opportunity to share the works you have created with the world. When you share your creative works online or in any other way, it is important for you to understand how copyright laws can protect your rights.

It is also important that young people understand other people's rights in their works. It is not okay for other people to use your creative works in a way that is unfair to you. And it is not okay for you to use other people's creative works in a way that is not fair to them.

No Harm Rationalization

Let's go through some copyright basics. Copyright law protects creative works. A creative work may be writing, music, a musical performance, a picture, a painting, software, or other permanent creation. If you create a work, then you are the owner of the copyright in that work. If a group of people creates a work, then everyone in the group is considered to be the owner of the copyright in that work.

If you create a work, it is automatically protected by copyright from the moment it is created. Most people use a copyright notice on their creative work. A copyright notice looks like this: © year of creation, creator's name. Copyright law protects a work even if it is published without a notice. But it is a good idea to include a copyright notice on your creative works so that everyone knows the work is yours and is protected by copyright.

When you are the owner of a copyright in a creative work, you have a variety of exclusive rights. The rights are called "exclusive" because you are the only one who can do these things with the work. The owner of the copyright has five exclusive rights:

1. The right to copy the work.

2. The right to distribute the work.

3. The right to modify the work.

4. The right to display the work.

5. The right to perform the work.

The copyright owner is the one who gets to decide whether to give permission for anyone else to do these five things with the work. This kind of permission is called a license. For example, you can decide to give others permission to copy your work or to display your work. You get to decide how long they can do this, how many copies they can make, whether or not they have to pay you, and so forth.

Here is how all of this might work in school. Let's imagine that you have created a work, such as a computer graphic or a poem. If your teacher wants to post it on the school Web site, he or she should request permission from you and your parents to post this work. Remember that you have the exclusive right to display the work, so if your teacher wants to display it, he or she should request permission—that is, a license—to display it.

If your work will be displayed on the school Web site, it is important for you to include your copyright notice. This notice should read: © year of creation, your name. You may want to retain all of your rights in your creative work. Or you may want to allow people to make and distribute copies of your work as long as they are not making any money from this. If you want to allow this kind of educational or nonprofit use, you can include a statement right next to the copyright notice that says: "Permission to copy and distribute for nonprofit or educational purposes is granted." This means that others may make and distribute copies as long as they are using the work for an educational or other nonprofit purpose and are not trying to make money from your work. Using this kind of permission statement is a nice way to use the Internet to share your creative work without giving up all of your rights.

You can also choose to give up all of your rights in your creative work. You do this by stating on the work that you are placing the work in the public domain. If you place your work in the public domain, that means that anyone can use your work in any way and that you no longer have any ownership or control over it. The other kinds of public domain works are those for which the copyright has expired and works created by the federal government.

The Copyright Rights of Others

Now let's consider the copyright rights of someone else who has created a work. If someone else has created a work, he or she owns the copyright to that work. The creator has all the exclusive rights to the work. The creator may have granted a license to a publisher to make copies and distribute the work. A publisher spends money to make copies of the work available to the public. Income received for the work is divided between the publisher and the creator. This income helps support the costs of making the work available.

Most important, the income provides the ability for the creator to support himself or herself so that he or she can create more works. Anytime you make a copy of a creative work without paying for it, you are "taking" something from the person who created it. You are taking the income the creator expected to receive from the distribution of the work. If you appreciate someone's creative efforts enough to make a copy of the work, then you owe the creator for the enjoyment or benefit the work has provided you.

Fair Use of Copyrighted Works

Sometimes people can make limited use of a copyrighted work if it is considered fair use. The fair use exemption, which is included as part of the copyright law, was created to ensure that the copyright laws balanced the benefits to the creators and the benefits to society. There are some kinds of uses of creative works that are important for society. If individuals want to use a copyrighted work in a way that is considered a fair use, they can do so without getting permission from the copyright owner.

Several questions must be considered to determine whether the use of a copyrighted work would be considered fair. All of the following factors have to be considered together:

- **How is the copyrighted work being used?** It is not considered fair to use a work for a commercial purpose. But it might be considered fair to use a work for an educational purpose or to criticize or review the work.

- **What kind of work is being used?** It is considered more fair to use a factual work and less fair to use a highly creative work.

- **How much of the work is being used?** It is considered more fair to use only a limited amount of a work and less fair to use the entire work or a large portion of the work.

- **How will the use affect the market for the work or the potential income the creator expects to receive from the work?** It is considered more fair to use a work if the use will not affect the income the creator of the work expects to receive and less fair if the use will reduce the creator's income.

Here are some examples of fair uses and uses that are not fair.

- **Your teacher can probably make copies of a newspaper article to distribute in class.** This is probably an educational use exemption, but there are some limitations on this kind of use that your teacher must follow. Your teacher cannot purchase one book and make copies for every student in class unless permission has been granted to make such copies. Your teacher also cannot post the newspaper article on the school

Web site because this kind of use goes beyond classroom use permitted under the educational use exemption. Your teacher can link to the article on another site.

- **You can make a copy of some pages of a book to use when writing a research paper.** This is a research use exemption. You cannot copy an entire book without permission to do so. You may not post the pages of the book on the Internet. But you may include brief quotations from the book as part of your research paper. And you may post your research paper on the Internet.

- **You may use up to 10 percent, but no more than 30 seconds, of recorded music as part of a multimedia presentation you show in class.** This is an educational use exemption. But you may not post this multimedia presentation on the Internet because this kind of use goes beyond classroom use. You can reproduce the lyrics

New World Rationalization

of a popular song as part of a report discussing the influence of music on teenagers. This is a review-and-criticism exemption. You may post this report on the Internet.

Copyright in the Information Age

Computer technologies and other kinds of technologies, like copy machines, make it much easier to make copies of someone else's copyrighted work. Many times when you copy a work, it is just as good as the original. Most people understand that when they make a copy of a creative work without permission from the creator or publisher, this is wrong.

But new technologies make it easier for people to rationalize that they are not doing anything wrong.

Sometimes people think that just because they can make copies without getting caught and punished, it is okay to do so. These people are using the No Consequences Rationalization. In these cases, the Is There a Rule? Test should be used. There is a rule against making copies of a copyrighted work. The rule protects the rights of creators, and shows that we value people's creative efforts.

Sometimes people think it is okay to make copies because everyone else does. This is the Follow the Crowd Rationalization. Other people might argue that they are just making one personal copy, so they are not really hurting the creator. This is the Little Bit Rationalization. In these instances, use the If Everybody Did It Test. If lots of people are making one copy, then the combined harm to the creator can be very great.

Some people argue that the Internet has created a new situation and that copyright laws are not appropriate or do not apply in

this setting. This is the New World Rationalization. If copyright laws are no longer appropriate, how will creators be paid for their efforts? Do you think that the government should pay creators? If the government pays creators, then government has control over what gets created. Do you think rich people should pay creators? Then rich people will have the control. Should advertisers pay creators? Then advertisers will have the control.

The best way to support the creation of new works is for the people who appreciate those works to recognize their responsibility to pay the creators of those works. The only way that people—including you—can make sure that the kinds of works they want to see created are created is to make sure that they are responsibly paying creators for their efforts.

It is true that the new technologies are changing some of the ways that creative works are distributed. Because of the Internet, creators now have greater ability to distribute their works directly to the people who want them without going through a publisher. The

Ghandi Test

direct relationships that can be formed between creators and people who appreciate their works will result in tremendous benefit to everyone—but only if people respect creators and treat their creative works responsibly.

Use the Gandhi Test in these situations. Your decisions about respecting the copyright rights of others are important in creating the kind of world where many people have the opportunity to be creators. Also use the Golden Rule Test. You can also be a creator. How do you want other people to treat your creative works?

Using Copyrighted Materials in School

It is important to respect the copyright rights of others when you are using copyrighted materials in school. It is a violation of copyright law and the school's Internet use policy to download copyrighted software, music, or computer games unless you have express permission from the copyright owner to do so. (You should also check your school policy to see if downloading such files is okay.)

The rules for the following categories of use apply if you want to copy, distribute, or place material that has been created by someone else on the school's public Web site or if you want to use material you have found on the Internet in class.

- **Public domain materials.** If a creative work is clearly in the public domain, you may freely make and distribute copies of the work or place it on the school Web site. But you must be sure that the work is in the public domain.

- **General permission.** If there is a notice included with the work that states that the

kind of use you propose is okay, this is considered general permission.

- **Fair use.** You should check with your teacher to see whether your proposed use falls within the fair use guidelines. It is not considered fair use to post materials on the Web for educational purposes. It may be considered fair use if you use a very limited portion of a work for the purposes of review or criticism.

- **Specific permission.** If you do not know what you can or cannot do with a particular work, the best approach is to ask permission from the creator of the work. Fortunately, with material found on the Internet it is usually easy to send the creator an e-mail message specifying how you propose to use the work and requesting permission to do so. Here is an example of a request for permission:

Subject: Request for Permission to Copy Material

Dear (name):

I am a student at (name of school). I would like to use (describe the material) (describe how you will use the material). I will properly reference your ownership of the material by (describe how). May I have your permission to use your material in this way? I need to have your answer by (date).

For the Teacher

Activity 1

1. Napster, the music downloading company, and its Web site have recently been involved in a variety of lawsuits concerning copyright violation. However, there is considerable debate as to whether the Napster Web site violates copyrights. Divide students into two groups—one group who argues that downloading music from the Internet is a violation of copyright and one group who argues that it is not a copyright violation.

2. Have students use the Internet or other information sources to research Napster-related debates and the lawsuits.

3. Have team members meet in a cooperative learning environment to share what they have learned and to devise a debate strategy.

4. Lead a class debate, or ask students to write an essay about what they learned.

Activity 2

Have students put themselves in the place of a graphic artist. Ask them to assume that they have just created some unique images and now want to find out what they should do to fully protect the copyright rights for their image. (Hint: Have students look at http://www.loc.gov/copyright.)

Activity 3

1. Have students conduct a poll of their fellow students with respect to use of pirated software. Ask them to draft a questionnaire they can pass out to their fellow students. The survey should ask questions about how often students use software that has not been purchased and whether they know of other individuals who engage in such activities.

2. After students have collected their data, have them create Excel graphs and present their findings to the class. (A PowerPoint presentation might be effective.)

3. After students have made their presentations, lead a discussion about ways to prevent people from using copyrighted software they did not pay for.

Activity 4

Invite an author, musician, or artist to come to your classroom to explain how he or she earns a living through the creation of new works.

UNIT 11

Watch Where You Are Looking

Max finds a Web site that has stories and pictures of adults and teens engaging in sexual activities. Most of the stories and pictures involve some kind of sexual activity. Max decides to download some of the stories and pictures and send them to friends. What are the possible consequences of such actions?

Darkside Sites

It probably comes as no surprise to you that adults are concerned about young people accessing some material that has been placed on the Internet. The sites your school is most concerned about are the darkside sites. These sites contain pornography and other profane and obscene materials, hate material and violent games, and information about dangerous or unhealthy activities. The material on darkside sites reflects a negative side of human nature. These sites promote violence and hatred. They foster sexual and racial harassment and disregard for the rights of others. They encourage crude attitudes. The individuals creating these sites simply do not share a vision of the world as a peaceful place where all people and other living things are treated with care and respect.

Inadvertent Access

It is also possible to mistakenly access material that is prohibited under the Internet use policy. Because your Web activities are monitored, it is important that you report any occasion when you access unacceptable material by mistake. Reporting will protect you against a claim that you intentionally violated the policy.

Here are some steps to take to avoid accessing inappropriate material by mistake:

- **Read, think, then click.** Be careful whenever you click on a link that will take you to a new site. When you conduct a search using a search tool, you may receive search results that could lead you to material that is not okay to access. It is important to read the search result description carefully before you click on the link. It is also important to Read, Think, Then Click if you are following links that are on a Web site. If you do not have a good idea where a link will take you, it is best not to click on it.

- **Type, check, then click.** Be very careful when you type URLs. Sites with darkside material sometimes use a domain name similar to the domain name of a popular site. The darkside site owners hope that people will access their site by mistake. Make sure you use the correct domain name. Get into the habit of always checking the domain name after you have typed it and before you click to access the site.

- **Turn it off and tell.** If you get to the wrong place, immediately turn off your screen and ask a teacher or computer lab monitor for help. Some sites with darkside material use a technology that can trap your browser into accessing more material on their sites or linking to another site with inappropriate material. Some sites disable your "back" button so that you cannot back out of the site. The best first response is to quickly turn off your screen and tell a teacher or a lab monitor. If you go to the wrong place but get out without requiring help, you should still report it to your teacher or lab monitor. The school monitors all student Web activity. By reporting that you have accessed inappropriate material by mistake, you will protect yourself against a complaint that you purposely accessed the material.

- **Read between the lines.** Some sites fostering violence and hatred appear to be acceptable sites. Their messages of hatred are disguised. But if you read closely, you will recognize their underlying messages.

Intentional Access

When you use the Internet at school, any intentional effort to access material that the policy prohibits will result in disciplinary action. Sometimes students think that they can get away with accessing this kind of material because nobody is watching them. You should be aware that some schools do monitor student Web use and can detect access to inappropriate material.

With all of the fuss adults have been making about "porn" on the Internet, many young people are going to be curious to see what is really out there. Curiosity is no excuse for violating school policy or your parents' rules!

Looking into the Mirror

While the Internet can be an eye to the world, it can also be a mirror that lets you take a closer look at yourself. Unfortunately, there are people in this world who think that combining sex with violence is an exciting or cool thing to do. Some people think that abusing others is fun. What kind of a person are you? If you watch where you are looking, you can get a good idea of the kind of a person you are. What you look at reflects on you—your values and your interests. What you think and how you think other people should be treated are important.

Use the Trusted Adult Test. Does what you look at on the Internet reflect the values that are important to the adults who are important in your life? Use the Check Inside Test. If you check inside and don't like what you see when you look into the mirror of what you look at on the Internet, please talk with a teacher, school counselor, or trusted adult.

For the Teacher

Activity 1

Have students create several lists of the kinds of materials that are on the Internet. Have them group the material into the following categories:

• Material that no young person and no adult should ever access.

• Material that is not appropriate for young people to access but may be acceptable for adults to access.

• Material that is generally not appropriate to access but may be appropriate to look at for research purposes.

• Material that is not appropriate to access when students are using the Internet at school for educational purposes.

Compare the lists the students created to the kinds of materials listed in the school's Internet use policy. How are the lists alike and how are they different?

Activity 2

Ask students to write an essay or engage in a debate addressing the following issue: Many people believe that filtering or blocking software should be used whenever children and teenagers use the Internet. Do you agree or disagree? Why?

UNIT 12

Don't Take Candy from Strangers

Amy has met a special friend in an online chat room. At first, she and the friend communicated about music groups, school, and life in general. Amy was happy to find someone who understood the problems she was having with parents and friends. More recently, Amy's friend has been asking her about sexual activities and sexual interests. Amy's friend wants to get together in person with her. As Amy's friend, what advice would you give her?

Do you remember when your parents taught you not to accept candy from a stranger? This is still a good rule for the Internet. Just as in real life, there are unsafe strangers on the Internet.

There are several different kinds of unsafe strangers on the Internet. They include the following:

• **Sexual Predators.** Sexual predators seek out young people and attempt to engage them in sexual talk. Some may even try to entice young people to meet with them in person.

• **Hate Group Recruiters.** Some people use the Internet as a hate tool to spread hate propaganda and recruit young people into organizations that foster hatred, violence, and intimidation of others on the basis of some perceived "difference."

- **Scam Artists.** Some people use the Internet in an attempt to scam and defraud others. Virtually all the "make a quick buck" schemes advertised on the Internet are fraudulent.

- **Cyberstalkers.** Cyberstalkers use the Internet to try to intimidate and harass other people. Sometimes a cyberstalker may know the person he or she is harassing, and the online harassment is related to a real-world personal dispute. At other times, cyberstalkers are strangers. A sexual predator, hate group recruiter, or scam artist may become a cyberstalkers if his or her initial contacts are not successful.

Sexual predators, hate group recruiters, and scam artists use the online equivalent of "candy." They write sweet things. They make sweet promises. They try to make their victims feel very comfortable communicating with them. This behavior is called *grooming*. The victim is being groomed to become willing to do something that he or she would not otherwise want to do. Through grooming, predators also set their victims up so that they might feel guilty about turning the person in. Cyberstalkers, on the other hand, do not use "candy." They use abusive, hurtful, and threatening language.

Sexual Predators

If you communicate with someone online who wants you to talk about sex, you will probably not know who this person is and what this person's motives are. You cannot be sure that this person is telling the truth. You may think you are communicating with someone your own age. But the other person may actually be an older person who is preying on you.

Some predators try to make contact with their victims in the real world. The predator has fed the young person so much "candy" that he or she is willing to trust the predator. This gives the predator a lot of control. Young people have been raped and sexually abused by predators they met online. Do not let this happen to you.

Teenage activism can help address the problem of predators on the Internet. One reason online predators can get away with their activities is that most of their victims just cut off the communication and try to forget that it occurred. Since there is little risk of punishment, predators simply move from one victim to another until they find someone who is very vulnerable.

If more teenagers reported predator contacts, the risk of punishment for the predator

Real World Test

would be greater. If a predator contacts you, recognize that you are probably not the only person this predator has contacted. Other teenagers may be more vulnerable or less able to assess potential danger than you are. Other teenagers may make the mistake of meeting with a predator in person. Your "smarts" and prompt action may help others who are more at risk than you are.

Hate Group Recruiters

There has been a rise in the presence of hate groups on the Internet. Hate groups attract people who think that their particular racial or religious group is, or should be, considered superior to others. Hate groups disseminate propaganda that criticizes or denigrates other people based on their religion, race, ethnicity, sexual orientation, or other characteristics.

Hate group recruiters specifically target young people to try to draw them into their groups. Young people who are most vulnerable to this are those who feel angry and left out in their real world. The message of the hate group recruiter is: "We love you. Other people don't. We are your true friends. Other people are your enemies." In fact, hate group recruiters do not love you. They simply are trying to draw you into their hate activities.

Hate groups sometimes have highly attractive, well-designed Web sites that create the impression that the group is legitimate and is presenting accurate information. These sites may contain material, such as rock music, that is of special interest to young people. But the rock music may be filled with messages of hatred, violence, and

Trusted Adult Test

intolerance. Hate groups also send unsolicited mass-mailings of hate literature with links to their sites.

Sometimes hate group members will specifically target a discussion group. Several members of the hate group will collaborate in sending messages to make it appear to others that there is widespread acceptance of the group's ideas. If any other discussion group participant indicates approval of the ideas expressed, one of the hate group recruiters will begin a private conversation with this participant to further encourage his or her participation with the hate group.

Scam Artists

There has been a significant growth in Internet fraud. By using the Internet, scam artists can make themselves appear very legitimate. The message from scam artists is generally something like, "Have I got a deal for you!" But the deal a scam artist offers will result in money for the scam artist and an empty bag for his or her victim.

Generally, victims of scam artists are adults. But young people are increasingly able to obtain debit cards or find other ways to send money to scam artists. The easier it is for young people to send money to scam artists, the more scam artists will target them.

The best advice for avoiding online scams is to remember that anything that sounds too good to be true is probably a scam.

Cyberstalkers

Cyberstalkers are people who use the Internet to stalk another person. Stalking generally involves repeated harassing or threatening behavior, such as repeatedly sending abusive e-mail messages. In many cases, the cyberstalker and the victim have had a prior relationship in the real world or online. Cyberstalking often begins when the victim has tried to cut off the relationship. The cyberstalker's intention is to maintain some form of control over the victim. Cyberstalking behavior can range from annoying to very threatening. There are federal and state laws against cyberstalking.

Cyberstalkers can also post messages someplace on the Internet that can result in harassment directed your way. For example, a cyberstalker may post a message in a chat room, providing your personal contact information and suggesting that other people contact you. Unfortunately, cyberstalkers have many ways they can use the Internet to find personal information on their victims.

Some people dismiss concerns about cyberstalking because it is something that just occurs through a computer. But the annoyance and fear caused by cyberstalking is just the same as stalking in the real world. When a person is being stalked, there is a constant feeling that the world is not safe. Sometimes cyberstalking can be associated with real-world violence.

Rules for Your Safety

It is possible that a predator, hate group recruiter, scam artist, or cyberstalker may contact you through your school account or personal account. The following rules are important to protect your personal safety:

- **Never give out personal contact information, such as your address, telephone number, work address, or your parent's work address or telephone number.** If you have a personal account, do not post personal contact information as part of your user profile.

- **Never agree to meet with someone you have met online without checking with your parents.** If your parents agree to have you meet with someone, be sure the meeting is held in a public place and have your parent accompany you to the meeting.

- **Be extra cautious if you are communicating with a person who appears to be attempting to conceal his or her true identity.**

- **Never judge anything on the Internet by initial appearances.** Regardless of how professional or impressive a Web site or e-mail message appears, this does not mean that the people who generated the site or messages are reputable.

- **If you receive unwanted contact that is merely annoying, send a message to the person, making it clear that you want**

him or her to stop contacting you. If the person does not stop and you are at home, tell your parents. If you are in school, tell your teacher or the computer lab monitor. You or an adult can contact this person's Internet Service Provider (ISP). ISPs have policies that prohibit the use of their systems to abuse another person, and the ISP can terminate the offender's account if provided with evidence of the offensive messages.

• **Tell your parent, teacher, or some other trusted person if you have become engaged in discussions that make you feel uncomfortable or have received harassing, threatening, abusive, or predatory messages.** If someone is abusing you or making you feel uncomfortable online, it is not your fault. It may have taken you a while to recognize that you might be communicating with a predator. Predators are frequently very good at moving slowly and trying to build up trust. You may feel embarrassed about some of your communications. But what is most important is getting this person out of your life. So, even if you are embarrassed, ask for help.

• **If you receive an inappropriate message, do not delete it.** Save the message as evidence that can be used to find the person responsible. (If you have mistakenly deleted some messages, they can probably be retrieved through the district or ISP back-up system.)

• **If you have received harassing, threatening, abusive, or predatory messages, ask a trusted adult to help you contact your local law enforcement officials, your closest Federal Bureau of Investigation (FBI) office, or the Center for Missing and Exploited Children (http://www.ncmec.org).** If you have been the victim of Internet fraud, ask an adult to help you file a fraud complaint with the Internet Fraud Complaint Center (http://www.ifccfbi.gov).

The Check Inside Test can help you to stay safe when dealing with dangerous strangers on the Internet. If something inside you feels like something is wrong, it probably is. Listen very closely to your internal feelings.

Check Inside Test

For the Teacher

Activity 1

Ask students to participate in some role-playing exercises in which pairs of students play the role of friends. Have them act out some scenarios in front of the class. Here are three hypothetical situations, but you may create many more.

1. Friend A has met an interesting person in a chat room and wants to meet the cyberfriend in person. Friend A tells Friend B that he or she is thinking about giving the cyberfriend personal contact information, such as a phone number and address so that a meeting time can be arranged. Have Friend B give Friend A advice on how to proceed.

2. Two of Jane's friends are discussing the fact that Jane is going to the airport to meet a person she met online. Jane made her two friends promise that they would not tell her parents or teachers about her meeting. The two friends are now discussing whether they should keep their promise and not tell anyone, or whether they should break their promise because they fear for Jane's safety.

3. Bill walked into his younger brother's room and noticed that he had been viewing a racial hate site. Bill does not know what to say to his younger brother. Have Bill ask his friend for advice on how to proceed.

Activity 2

Have students write an essay on the following questions: Why do you think sexual predators, scam artists, and hate groups use the Internet? What advantages does the Internet give these groups? What can you do to take these advantages away?

Activity 3

Have students draft a sample e-mail designed to cut off contact with groups or individuals with whom they no longer want to have correspondence.

UNIT 13

Don't Go Where You Don't Belong

Max hacked into a computer at the local bank. He just wanted to try to do it without getting caught. Max did not change anyone's account balances or manipulate any records. Even though Max was "just having fun," do you think there is anything wrong or risky about his actions?

Computer Security Violations

Attempting to break into someone else's computer system is against the law. Breaking into someone's Web site and posting material is against the law. Intentionally creating and sending a computer virus is against the law.

All of these activities are considered to be computer security violations, frequently called *hacking*. The reason these activities are against the law is that they cause substantial harm to others. What kind of harm? Financial loss. Disruption of business or organizational activities. Loss of privacy and release of confidential information. Loss of confidence in the Internet. Here is what Louis J. Freeh, director of the Federal Bureau of

Investigation, told a Senate Judiciary Committee about cybercrime on March 28, 2000:

> Over the past several years we have seen a range of computer crimes ranging from defacement of Web sites by juveniles to sophisticated intrusions that we suspect may be sponsored by foreign powers, and everything in between. Some of these are obviously more significant than others. The

theft of national security information from a government agency or the interruption of electrical power to a major metropolitan area have greater consequences for national security, public safety, and the economy than the defacement of a Web site. But even the less serious categories have real consequences and, ultimately, can undermine confidence in e-commerce and violate privacy or property rights. A Web site hack that shuts down an e-commerce site can have disastrous consequences for a business. An intrusion that results in the theft of credit card numbers from an online vendor can result in significant financial loss and, more broadly, reduce consumers' willingness to engage in e-commerce. Because of these implications, it is critical that we have in place the programs and resources to investigate and, ultimately, to deter these sorts of crimes.
(http://www.cybercrime.gov/freeh328.htm)

Young people who engage in hacking have different reasons for their actions. Some hackers think that hacking is a way to increase their computer skills. Others think that it is a kind of competition or game. They try to break into as many computer systems as they can. Then they "leave their mark" to show other hackers that they have been there. Some hackers may not like a particular technology company. They want to demonstrate the security problems with the company's products. Other hackers may want to protest the actions of a company or government agency. They engage in "hacktivism" by breaking into a company's or government's Web site and posting offensive material. Some hackers steal credit card numbers to purchase products.

Sometimes young people interested in computers join online computer discussion groups. These groups are a place to make friends and discuss technical issues.

Unfortunately, some of these groups think that it is, or should be, okay for people to engage in hacking. Participants in these groups give rationalizations for why hacking should be considered okay. The following are some rationalizations hackers commonly use:

"Breaking into a system does not cause any harm. It's just a game. Nobody gets hurt. It's not like breaking into a house."

This is the No Harm Rationalization. These hackers try to deny that their actions cause any harm. It is easy to make this rationalization because hackers are not in a position to actually see the harm they have caused. It is true that breaking into a computer system does not feel the same as breaking into a house.

The fact is that whenever someone tries to break into a computer system, it is definitely not a game for the company or government agency that manages the computer security system. Computer security professionals do not have any way to determine whether the individual trying to break into their system is a bored teenager who is just having a little fun or a criminal or terrorist who is intent on breaking into the system for extremely harmful purposes. Break-ins and attempted break-ins cause significant disruption and loss.

Let's try the Golden Rule Test on this rationalization. If you now have sufficient computer skills to engage in computer hacking, you may in the future be a computer professional responsible for maintaining the security of a system. Imagine how you would feel if you had to spend a lot of time responding to attempted break-ins by a bunch of bored teens. If you are unable to imagine yourself in such a position, consider another Golden Rule Test. How would you feel if someone broke into your house or car?

How would you feel if someone accessed your personal e-mail account?

"It's a new world. Old world rules have no place on the Internet."

This is the New World Rationalization. It may be a new world, and some rules may change. But concepts of privacy, ownership, and appropriate boundaries have not disappeared. While we can expect to see some changes in some rules, it is highly unlikely that people will ever consider it acceptable for a person to invade someone else's private computer system.

Let's try the If Everybody Did It Test. How well do you think the Internet would function if everybody were trying to break into every computer system connected through the Internet?

Or let's try the Gandhi Test. Do you think that one of the rules of the new world should be that sophisticated techies should have the right to break into any computer they want to just because they can?

"I'm doing the owner of the computer system a favor by demonstrating problems with security. The owner should be grateful. It's not my fault that the system has bad security or that the owner bought a product from a company that sells faulty software."

This is an interesting combination of the Finger of Blame and the Good Intentions Rationalizations. Not only do hackers try to shift the blame to the victim, they also argue that they are doing something beneficial.

Consider this rationalization using the Real World Test. How would you feel if someone broke into your locker and then told you they were checking to see whether your lock worked and then told you it was your fault because you bought a cheap lock? If owners of computer systems want to have their security checked, they can hire someone to do this job in a way that protects the confidentiality of the data on their system. The fact that some software companies sell products that are not as secure as they should be does not justify causing problems for the companies or government agencies that purchase those products.

"By figuring out how to gain access to computer systems, I'm increasing my computer skills. This will make me a better employee."

This is a Good Intentions Rationalization. It is true that, in the past, hacking was seen as a way to advance in the technology field. And, yes, many of today's technology millionaires got their start as hackers. But the world has changed. As more and more companies and government agencies use technologies that enhance their operations, the security of computer systems has taken on greater

If Everybody Did It Test

importance. Hacking is no longer viewed as an appropriate way to gain computer skills.

Try using the Check Inside Test. Do you really think that engaging in illegal activity is a good way to achieve your career goals? There are many excellent ways to enhance your skills in the use of technology. Talk to your teacher or school counselor about these opportunities. Employers today want to hire people who have the self-control to use technology legally and ethically. They do not want employees who think that it is okay to violate the law.

"I'm a modern-day Robin Hood. I will seek out evidence of corruption by corporations and people in power. I will use my skills to disrupt their activities and reveal evidence of their corruption."

This is another combination of the Finger of Blame and the Good Intentions Rationalizations. "Brilliant but mischievous,

Good Intentions Rationalization

school kids save the world by hacking into a computer system!" It only happens this way in the movies. In real life, people who are successful in revealing corruption by companies or governments do not use computer hacking as a method.

Try using the Gandhi Test. If you intend to fight corruption in the world, do you think you can be successful by engaging in criminal behavior? Or do you think you will be more successful if you uphold high ethical standards for your behavior?

If you are trying to make the world a better place, there are many effective ways to use the communication and information-sharing capabilities of the Internet. People who are successful in creating positive change can use the Internet to find and share information with others who have similar concerns. You will be far more effective in addressing problems in the world if you maintain high ethical standards for your own behavior.

Learn how to use the Internet in a positive way to make the world a better place. Recognize that there are career or public service opportunities for people who want to use their computer skills to address corruption or create positive social change. Talk with your school counselor and local legal authorities about the kinds of skills required for such careers.

"They will never catch or punish me."

This is not true. (And even if it were true, are you going to go through life making decisions based on whether or not someone is going to catch and punish you?)

Use the Is There a Rule? Test. All of the activities described in this unit are illegal. The reason the actions are considered illegal is that they cause serious harm to others. Anyone who engages in criminal activities related to computer security is risking jail time. You can find out more about law enforcement's efforts to address cybercrime at the U.S. Department of Justice Web site at http://www.cybercrime.gov/.

A Better Option

If you know a lot about computers, recognize that there are many ways you can expand your knowledge and use your skills to help other people. Here are just a few ideas:

- **Join a student technology program.** Many schools have established student technology programs to train and use students for technical support in the schools. If your school does not have such a program, work with other students and teachers to create one.

- **Nonprofit social service organizations and community centers could use your assistance with their computer systems.**

New World Rationalization

You could volunteer to help them upgrade their systems. Or you could help them create or maintain a Web site.

- **Some communities have established community technology centers for people who do not have the resources or skills to use the Internet.** These organizations may need assistance in establishing community Web pages, repairing older donated equipment, providing network support, or providing training to new users.

- **If you do not like how some companies develop and provide software or Internet products, use your technical skills to further the development of alternative approaches.**

- **If you are angry about something that is happening in the world, create your own protest Web site.** But be sure you engage in responsible protest and not in online pollution. Do your homework. Do not use inflammatory language. Do not engage in personal attacks or defame others. Focus on the facts and provide an intelligent analysis of the problem. If you want to be a rebel, that is fine. But be an effective, responsible rebel.

You will find the challenges involved with beneficial projects such as these much more exciting and rewarding than hiding in your room and trying to break into somebody's computer system.

For the Teacher

Activity 1

Have students consider the following three computer security violations:

1. Max finds a security hole in the computer system of a company that sells products on the Internet. He is able to access the company's database. The database contains credit card numbers of the company's customers. Max uses some of the credit cards to make online purchases.

2. A software company has just released a new version of server software. Amy investigates the new server software by trying to penetrate the computers of companies that have installed the server software. Amy finds a security hole and develops an executable file to penetrate the hole. She posts this file on an anonymous Web site. She then sends anonymous messages to several hacker newsgroups providing information about where the file can be found.

3. Max has become an environmental activist. He is very angry about the activities of a company he believes is creating significant pollution in a Third World country. Max successfully hacks into the company's Web site and posts protest materials on the site.

Instruct students to play the role of one of the "victims" of the computer security violations described in the previous three scenarios. The possible victims include the company selling products on the Internet, a customer of the company selling products on the Internet, an executive of the software company, or an executive of a company using the software provided by the software company. Have students write a letter to Max or Amy describing the impact of the computer security violations. (Examples of letters written by "real victims" will be posted on the Responsible Netizen Web site at http://netizen.uoregon.edu).

Activity 2

Invite a representative from the U.S. Department of Justice, the local police, or a local technology company to come to your class to discuss cybercrime issues.

UNIT 14

Do Your Part

*A*my is a member of a
high school Student Technology
Club. She became aware of a plan to
establish a community technology
center at a local facility that provides
afterschool care for elementary
students. She is now developing
plans for the Student Technology
Club to provide technical
assistance and other help for
the community technology
center. Can you think of any
ways you could help your community
in a similar fashion?

Do Your Part in the School System

All users of the school's computer system
have a responsibility to maintain the security
of the system and to respect the limitations of
the computer resources.

Account Security. Your primary
responsibility is for the security of your
personal account. Your account is a doorway
into the school's computer system. You are
responsible for keeping your doorway secure.
Here are some ways to do that:

- **Choose a password that includes both
  letters and numbers (or characters).**
  Don't choose a password that someone who
  knows you could easily guess. Change your
  password whenever the technology
  coordinator requests that you do so.

- **Don't share your password with other
  students.**

- **If you are asked to provide a password to enter a Web site, don't use your account password.** Choose another password.

Computer Viruses. You must be careful not to introduce a computer virus into the school network. Computer viruses are programs that can destroy other programs or data. Here is some important information on viruses:

- **Never open an e-mail attachment unless you are absolutely sure you know the sender and the contents of the attachment.** Many viruses are distributed via e-mail attachments.

- **Deliberate attempts to disrupt system performance or data by knowingly spreading a computer virus is considered to be a criminal activity under both state and federal laws.** If you engage in this activity, the school will contact the local legal authorities and cooperate with them in their investigation of your activities.

Golden Rule Test

Security Problems. It is possible that you may accidentally stumble into a security problem. Take these precautions:

- **If you identify a possible security problem, immediately notify your school or the school's technology coordinator.** It will be helpful if you can provide information about how you identified the problem.

- **Do not demonstrate the security problem to anyone other than a technology coordinator.**

- **Do not go looking for security problems.** This will be treated as an unlawful attempt to gain unauthorized access to the computer system. If you attempt to gain unauthorized access to the school computer system, the school will contact the local legal authorities and cooperate with them in their investigation of your activities.

Resource Limits. There are limits to the resources on the school's computer system and the Internet. Students who misuse resources create problems for those who need access to educational activities. Any activity that creates a large amount of traffic, such as sending messages to a large number of people, should be avoided. Be sure to stay within your disk quota.

Do Your Part on the Internet

There are many ways you can do your part to make the Internet a better place for everyone who uses it. You may not yet have sufficient skills to do some of the following things, but you will gain these skills as you use the Internet.

- **Create a Web site that has value for others.** This may be a Web site that contains information about a subject you are interested in. You can provide links to other sites that provide information about this subject, as well as provide your own ideas and thoughts.

- **Help others create Web sites.** If you have good skills in creating Web sites, you can volunteer your services to nonprofit organizations in your community and help them create Web sites. You might also be able to help teachers who are creating their own classroom Web pages.

No Consequences Rationalization

- **Provide help to newbies you meet on the Internet.** A newbie is a new Internet user. If you realize that someone who has joined an online group isn't quite sure how to participate, you can send that individual a private message offering some suggestions.

- **If a flame war breaks out in a discussion group, try to be a peacemaker.** Try to help people discuss their differences of opinion without attacking each other. You may not be successful, but by trying to help you will be learning good communication skills.

- **If you notice something wrong or dangerous happening, don't just turn away.** Do what you can to help. If you recognize someone as a dangerous online stranger but one of your online friends does not, provide some words of warning. If you think that someone might be getting into a dangerous situation, discuss your concerns with an adult who can help. If you find something really wrong on the Internet or become aware of illegal activities, report this to the appropriate legal authorities.

- **Think globally.** Find places where you can interact with young people from other

nations. You will learn more about people in the world. You can also begin to work together from many parts of the world to resolve problems. Through the Internet, young people can be very effective players in helping to make this world a better place for everyone to live in.

Young people are playing a very important role in the emergence of the Internet. They have the power to help shape and mold both the Internet and the real world through the power of positive change. By using the Ethical Decision-Making Strategies described in this book, you can play an important role in this process.

For the Teacher

Activity 1

1. Have the class conduct a brainstorming session to create a list of ideas or activities for students to do their part in making a contribution to the Internet.

2. After the class has created a list, team up students with similar interests to pursue one of the projects. See the section "Do Your Part on the Internet" in this unit for some sample project ideas.

3. Have student groups draft a long-term project plan and set aside class time for group members to work on the project. This could be the culminating project in your ethics curriculum.

Activity 2

Lead a class discussion that answers the following questions:

- What do you think would happen if everyone knew your e-mail password? What would happen if you knew all your friends' passwords?

- Imagine you have just received an e-mail from someone you do not know. There is an interesting attachment titled "greatvacationspots.cvs" included in the e-mail. What should you do?

- What are the worst computer viruses you have heard of or experienced? What damage do the viruses do to a computer system?

Appendix

ISTE National Educational Technology Standards (NETS) and Performance Indicators for Students

The National Educational Technology Standards for students are divided into six broad categories. Standards within each category are to be introduced, reinforced, and mastered by students. These categories provide a framework for linking performance indicators, listed by grade level, to the standards. Teachers can use these standards and profiles as guidelines for planning technology-based activities in which students achieve success in learning, communication, and life skills.

1. Basic operations and concepts

- Students demonstrate a sound understanding of the nature and operation of technology systems.

- Students are proficient in the use of technology.

2. Social, ethical, and human issues

- Students understand the ethical, cultural, and societal issues related to technology.

- Students practice responsible use of technology systems, information, and software.

- Students develop positive attitudes toward technology uses that support lifelong learning, collaboration, personal pursuits, and productivity.

3. Technology productivity tools

- Students use technology tools to enhance learning, increase productivity, and promote creativity.

- Students use productivity tools to collaborate in constructing technology-enhanced models, preparing publications, and producing other creative works.

4. Technology communications tools

- Students use telecommunications to collaborate, publish, and interact with peers, experts, and other audiences.

- Students use a variety of media and formats to communicate information and ideas effectively to multiple audiences.

5. Technology research tools

- Students use technology to locate, evaluate, and collect information from a variety of sources.

- Students use technology tools to process data and report results.

- Students evaluate and select new information resources and technological innovations based on the appropriateness to specific tasks.

6. Technology problem-solving and decision-making tools

- Students use technology resources for

solving problems and making informed decisions.

- Students employ technology in the development of strategies for solving problems in the real world.

Profiles for Technology-Literate Students

All students should have opportunities to demonstrate the following performances. Numbers in parentheses following each performance indicator refer to the standards category to which the performance is linked.

Grades 6-8

Prior to completion of Grade 8 students will:

1. Apply strategies for identifying and solving routine hardware and software problems that occur during everyday use. (1)

2. Demonstrate knowledge of current changes in information technologies and the effect those changes have on the workplace and society. (2)

3. Exhibit legal and ethical behaviors when using information and technology, and discuss consequences of misuse. (2)

4. Use content-specific tools, software, and simulations (e.g., environmental probes, graphing calculators, exploratory environments, Web tools) to support learning and research. (3, 5)

5. Apply productivity/multimedia tools and peripherals to support personal productivity, group collaboration, and learning throughout the curriculum. (3, 6)

6. Design, develop, publish, and present products (e.g., Web pages, videotapes) using technology resources that demonstrate and communicate curriculum concepts to audiences inside and outside the classroom. (4, 5, 6)

7. Collaborate with peers, experts, and others using telecommunications and collaborative tools to investigate curriculum-related problems, issues, and information, and to develop solutions or products for audiences inside and outside the classroom. (4, 5)

8. Select and use appropriate tools and technology resources to accomplish a variety of tasks and solve problems. (5, 6)

9. Demonstrate an understanding of concepts underlying hardware, software, and connectivity, and of practical applications to learning and problem solving. (1, 6)

10. Research and evaluate the accuracy, relevance, appropriateness, comprehensiveness, and bias of electronic information sources concerning real-world problems. (2, 5, 6)

Grades 9-12

Prior to completion of Grade 12 students will:

1. Identify capabilities and limitations of contemporary and emerging technology resources and assess the potential of these systems and services to address personal, lifelong learning, and workplace needs. (2)

2. Make informed choices among technology systems, resources, and services. (1,2)

3. Analyze advantages and disadvantages of widespread use of and reliance on technology in the workplace and in society as a whole. (2)

4. Demonstrate and advocate for legal and ethical behavior among peers, family, and community regarding the use of technology and information. (2)

5. Use technology tools and resources for managing and communicating personal/professional information (e.g., finances, schedules, addresses, purchases, correspondence). (3, 4)

6. Evaluate technology-based options, including distance and distributed education, for lifelong learning. (5)

7. Routinely and efficiently use online information resources to meet needs for collaboration, research, publications, communications, and productivity. (4, 5, 6)

8. Select and apply technology tools for research, information analysis, problem solving, and decision making in content learning. (4, 5)

9. Investigate and apply expert systems, intelligent agents, and simulations in real-world situations. (3, 5, 6)

10. Collaborate with peers, experts, and others to contribute a content-related knowledge base by using technology to compile, synthesize, produce, and disseminate information, models, and other creative works. (4, 5, 6)